GOODSON MUMBA

SALES AND MARKETING SYNERGY

Driving Growth Together

Copyright © 2024 by Goodson Mumba

All rights reserved. No part of this publication may be reproduced, stored or transmitted in any form or by any means, electronic, mechanical, photocopying, recording, scanning, or otherwise without written permission from the publisher. It is illegal to copy this book, post it to a website, or distribute it by any other means without permission.

First edition

ISBN: 9798335227407

*This book was professionally typeset on Reedsy.
Find out more at reedsy.com*

Contents

	Preface	v
	Acknowledgement	viii
	Dedication	ix
	Disclaimer	x
1	Chapter 1: Understanding the Sales and Marketing Ecosystem	1
2	Chapter 2: Building a Strong Foundation	11
3	Chapter 3: Identifying Your Target Audience	22
4	Chapter 4: Crafting Your Brand Story	38
5	Chapter 5: Developing Effective Marketing Strategies	53
6	Chapter 6: Creating a Powerful Sales Strategy	70
7	Chapter 7: Aligning Sales and Marketing Teams	100
8	Chapter 8: Leveraging Data and Analytics	130
9	Chapter 9: Content Marketing for Sales Enablement	160
10	Chapter 10: Digital Marketing Strategies	191
11	Chapter 11: Enhancing Customer Experience	219
12	Chapter 12: Sales and Marketing Automation	232
13	Chapter 13: Managing Sales and Marketing Budgets	245
14	Chapter 14: Training and Development	258

15 Chapter 15: Measuring Success and Scaling Up	272
About the Author	286

Preface

In today's rapidly evolving business landscape, the synergy between sales and marketing is no longer a luxury—it's a necessity. As companies strive to remain competitive and drive growth, the alignment of these two critical functions has emerged as a powerful catalyst for success. This book, "Sales and Marketing Synergy: Driving Growth Together," aims to provide a comprehensive guide to harnessing the combined power of sales and marketing to achieve extraordinary results.

Over the years, I've had the privilege of working with numerous organizations across various industries, witnessing firsthand the transformative impact of a well-integrated sales and marketing strategy. Time and again, I've seen companies that embrace this synergy outperform their competitors, achieving higher revenue growth, greater customer satisfaction, and enhanced brand loyalty. However, I've also seen many organizations struggle with misalignment, leading to missed opportunities, inefficiencies, and stagnation.

"Sales and Marketing Synergy: Driving Growth Together" is born out of a desire to bridge this gap. It is designed for business leaders, sales and marketing professionals, and anyone looking to drive growth through effective collaboration. The book delves into the intricacies of aligning sales and marketing efforts, offering practical insights, real-world examples, and actionable strategies to create a cohesive and high-performing revenue-generating engine.

The journey begins with a deep dive into understanding the sales and marketing ecosystem, exploring their evolution, key differences, and common misconceptions. From there, we build a strong foundation by establishing core values, defining roles, and setting clear objectives. We then move into identifying target audiences, crafting compelling brand stories, and developing effective marketing and sales strategies. Each chapter is designed to provide you with the tools and knowledge needed to foster collaboration, leverage data and analytics, enhance customer experiences, and ultimately, drive growth.

Throughout this book, you'll find case studies and examples from leading companies that have successfully integrated their sales and marketing functions. These stories serve as both inspiration and proof that with the right approach, achieving sales and marketing synergy is not only possible but also immensely rewarding.

As you embark on this journey, I encourage you to approach the content with an open mind and a collaborative spirit. The path to sales and marketing synergy requires commitment, communication, and a willingness to embrace change. However, the rewards are well worth the effort, as you will discover new opportunities for growth, innovation, and long-term success.

Thank you for choosing to explore "Sales and Marketing Synergy: Driving Growth Together." I hope this book serves as a valuable resource and guide on your journey towards creating a powerful, integrated sales and marketing strategy that drives sustainable growth.

Best regards,

Goodson Mumba

Acknowledgement

I would like to eternally and gratefully acknowledge the Almighty God for the infinite intelligence from His universal mind where we draw from all that we come to know and are yet to know. May I also acknowledge and thank everyone that has played a part in my journey of life in terms of spiritual, moral, emotional and material support.

Dedication

I extend my sincerest gratitude to my beloved wife, Edith Mumba, and our children, Angelina, Lubuto, Letticia, Lulumbi, and Butusho, for their unwavering support and understanding throughout the conception, writing, and eventual publication of this book, despite the sacrifices and challenges they endured.

Disclaimer

This book is a work of fiction. Names, characters, businesses, places, events, and incidents are either the products of the author's imagination or used in a fictitious manner. Any resemblance to actual persons, living or dead, or actual events is purely coincidental.

1

Chapter 1: Understanding the Sales and Marketing Ecosystem

The Evolution of Sales and Marketing

In the bustling conference room of InnovateTech's headquarters, tension hung thick in the air. Emma, the Head of Marketing, and David, the Sales Director, sat on opposite ends of the long table, their expressions a mix of frustration and skepticism. They were gathered for a crucial meeting called by the CEO, Lisa, to address the company's stagnant growth and disjointed sales and marketing efforts.

As the meeting began, Lisa stood at the head of the table, her gaze sweeping over the room. "Thank you all for being here," she began, her tone serious yet determined. "It's no secret that we're facing challenges in driving growth. Our sales have plateaued, and our marketing efforts seem to be missing the mark. We need to figure out why."

Emma shifted uncomfortably in her chair, feeling the weight of responsibility on her shoulders. She knew that the disconnect between sales and marketing was a significant factor in their struggles, but she wasn't sure how to bridge the gap.

David, on the other hand, was all too familiar with the friction between their departments. He leaned forward, his voice edged with frustration. "It's like we're speaking different languages," he said, gesturing between himself and Emma. "Marketing comes up with these flashy campaigns, but they don't translate to actual sales."

Lisa nodded in understanding, her eyes flickering with determination. "I hear you," she said. "But I believe there's more to it than just miscommunication. We need to understand the history and evolution of sales and marketing to grasp why they're not working together as they should."

With that, she motioned to the screen at the front of the room, where a timeline of sales and marketing milestones appeared. From the advent of door-to-door salesmen to the rise of digital marketing, each era was marked with significant shifts in consumer behavior and communication channels.

"As you can see," Lisa continued, "sales and marketing have evolved dramatically over the years. But despite these changes, one thing remains constant: the need for synergy between the two. We need to learn from the past to shape our future."

Emma and David exchanged a glance, a spark of understanding flickering between them. Perhaps, they realized, their struggles were not unique but rather part of a broader narrative of transformation and adaptation in the world of business.

As the meeting drew to a close, Lisa left them with a challenge. "Let's use this knowledge to inform our approach moving forward," she said. "By understanding where we've come from, we can better navigate where we're going. Together."

Key Differences and Overlaps

As the sun dipped below the horizon, casting a warm glow over the city skyline, Emma and David found themselves seated across from each other in a cozy cafe, their laptops open and steaming mugs of coffee between them. They had decided to continue their discussion outside the confines of the office, hoping that a change of scenery might spark some fresh ideas.

David leaned forward, his brow furrowed in thought. "Alright, let's get down to it," he said, tapping his finger on the table. "What do you think are the key differences between sales and marketing?"

Emma considered the question for a moment, sipping her coffee as she organized her thoughts. "Well," she began, "I think one of the main differences is the timeframe. Marketing is focused on building long-term brand awareness and generating leads, while sales is more about closing deals and driving immediate revenue."

David nodded in agreement, jotting down notes on his laptop. "Right," he said. "And because of that difference in focus, there can sometimes be a disconnect between our goals and priorities."

Emma nodded, a flicker of understanding crossing her face. "Exactly," she said. "But I think there are also areas where our roles overlap. For example, both sales and marketing are ultimately trying to understand and meet the needs of the customer."

David smiled, impressed by Emma's insight. "You're absolutely right," he said. "And that's where the potential for synergy lies. If we can align our efforts to better serve the customer, we'll be unstoppable."

Their conversation continued late into the evening, as they brainstormed ideas for how to bridge the gap between their departments. By the time they parted ways, they had a renewed sense of purpose and a shared vision for the future of InnovateTech.

As they walked out into the cool night air, Emma couldn't help but feel a sense of optimism. She knew that transforming the relationship between sales and marketing wouldn't be easy, but she also knew that with David by her side, they could accomplish anything. Together, they would drive growth and usher in a new era of success for their company.

Importance of Integration

The next morning, Emma and David reconvened in Lisa's spacious office, where the morning sunlight streamed in through the floor-to-ceiling windows, casting a warm glow over the room. They were joined by Lisa herself, who had called the meeting to discuss the importance of integration between sales and marketing.

"Good morning, everyone," Lisa said, her voice tinged with enthusiasm. "I'm glad you could join me today to discuss this critical topic. As we've discussed, the divide between our sales and marketing teams has been holding us back. But I believe that by integrating our efforts, we can unlock a world of potential."

Emma and David exchanged a glance, a sense of determination shining in their eyes. They had spent hours brainstorming ideas the previous night, and they were eager to share their insights with Lisa.

"Integration is more than just aligning our goals and priorities," David said, leaning forward in his chair. "It's about breaking down the barriers between our departments and working together as a unified team."

Emma nodded in agreement, her mind racing with possibilities. "Exactly," she said. "By integrating our strategies and sharing insights, we can create a seamless experience for our customers from the first touchpoint to the final sale."

Lisa smiled, impressed by their passion and determination. "I couldn't agree more," she said. "But integration won't happen overnight. It will require a concerted effort from all of us, as well as a willingness to challenge the status quo."

With that, they launched into a discussion about practical steps they could take to integrate their sales and marketing efforts, from joint planning sessions to shared metrics and KPIs. By the end of the meeting, they had outlined a comprehensive plan that would lay the groundwork for a new era of collaboration and growth at InnovateTech.

As they filed out of Lisa's office, Emma and David shared a knowing smile. They knew that the road ahead wouldn't be easy, but they also knew that with Lisa's support and their shared commitment to integration, they could overcome any obstacle that stood in their way. Together, they would drive growth and propel InnovateTech to new heights of success.

Common Challenges and Misconceptions

The atmosphere in the conference room shifted as Lisa brought the discussion to the next critical point: common challenges and misconceptions plaguing the integration of sales and marketing.

With furrowed brows and thoughtful expressions, Emma, David, and the rest of the team listened intently as Lisa began, her voice calm yet firm, "Before we dive deeper into our strategies for integration, we need to address the elephant in the room—the challenges and misconceptions that have hindered our progress thus far."

Emma leaned forward, eager to hear Lisa's insights. "What challenges are you referring to?" she asked, her tone curious.

Lisa nodded, acknowledging the question. "One of the most common challenges is the perception that sales and marketing are fundamentally at odds with each other," she explained. "There's often a lack of trust and understanding between the two departments, which leads to siloed thinking and missed opportunities."

David nodded in agreement, his frustration evident. "It's true," he admitted. "There's this misconception that marketing is all about generating leads, while sales is solely responsible for closing deals. But the reality is much more nuanced than that."

Lisa nodded, her expression sympathetic. "Exactly," she said. "And that's why it's essential for us to challenge these misconceptions and foster a culture of collaboration and mutual respect between sales and marketing."

As the discussion continued, they delved into other common challenges, such as misaligned goals and priorities, lack of communication, and resistance to change. But with each challenge came an opportunity for growth and transformation, and Emma felt a renewed sense of determination to overcome them.

As the meeting drew to a close, Lisa left them with a powerful message: "We may face challenges along the way, but I believe that by working together with transparency, empathy, and a shared vision, we can overcome any obstacle that stands in our way. Let's embrace this opportunity to drive growth together."

With those words ringing in their ears, Emma, David, and the rest of the team left the conference room feeling inspired and ready to tackle the challenges ahead. They knew that the road to integration wouldn't be easy, but they also knew that with Lisa's leadership and their collective determination, they could achieve anything. Together, they would drive growth and usher in a new era of success for InnovateTech.

Industry Trends and Innovations

The air in the conference room buzzed with anticipation as Lisa, the CEO of InnovateTech, prepared to address the team about the importance of staying abreast of industry trends and innovations in sales and marketing.

With a click of her remote, Lisa brought up a vibrant slide deck showcasing the latest trends and cutting-edge innovations in the field. The room was illuminated by the glow of the screen as she began, her voice filled with excitement and enthusiasm.

"As we navigate the ever-evolving landscape of sales and marketing, it's crucial for us to stay ahead of the curve and adapt to emerging trends and innovations," Lisa began, her eyes shining with passion. "The world is changing rapidly, and we need to change with it if we want to remain competitive."

Emma and David exchanged eager glances, their curiosity piqued by the promise of new insights and ideas. They knew that understanding industry trends and innovations was key to driving growth and staying ahead of the competition.

As Lisa delved into the presentation, she highlighted a myriad of trends shaping the sales and marketing landscape, from the rise of AI-powered chatbots and virtual assistants to the growing importance of personalization and customer experience.

"With advancements in technology and shifts in consumer behavior, we have more opportunities than ever before to connect with our audience in meaningful ways," Lisa explained, her voice filled with conviction. "But it's essential for us to embrace these trends and leverage them to our advantage."

David nodded in agreement, his mind racing with possibilities. "Absolutely," he said. "We need to be proactive in adopting new technologies and strategies that can help us better understand our customers and meet their needs."

Emma chimed in, her voice eager. "And by staying informed about industry trends and innovations, we can position ourselves as thought leaders in our field and drive innovation within our own company," she added.

As the meeting drew to a close, Lisa left them with a challenge: "Let's make a commitment to staying ahead of the curve and embracing change as we continue our journey of growth and innovation. Together, we can achieve anything."

With those words echoing in their minds, Emma, David, and

the rest of the team left the conference room feeling inspired and energized. They knew that by embracing industry trends and innovations, they could unlock a world of potential and drive InnovateTech to new heights of success. Together, they would lead the charge into the future of sales and marketing.

Case Studies of Successful Integration

As the discussion in the conference room continued, Lisa, the CEO of InnovateTech, shifted the focus to real-world examples of successful integration between sales and marketing teams. She brought up a series of case studies, each highlighting companies that had overcome challenges similar to their own and achieved remarkable results through collaboration and synergy.

With a click of her remote, Lisa displayed the first case study on the screen—a story of a software company that had transformed its sales and marketing operations through a holistic approach to integration.

"As we embark on our own journey of integration, it's essential for us to learn from the successes of others," Lisa began, her voice filled with determination. "These case studies serve as inspiration and guidance as we strive to drive growth together."

Emma and David leaned forward, their eyes fixed on the screen as they absorbed the details of each case study. They were struck by the diverse range of industries and companies represented, from small startups to multinational corporations, all united by their commitment to breaking down silos and fostering collaboration between sales and marketing.

"These case studies demonstrate that integration isn't just a buzzword—it's a proven strategy for driving tangible results," Lisa continued, her voice ringing with conviction. "By working together, we can achieve far more than we ever could alone."

David nodded in agreement, his mind racing with ideas inspired by the success stories before them. "Absolutely," he said. "These case studies show us that integration isn't just about aligning our goals and priorities—it's about leveraging each other's strengths to create something truly extraordinary."

Emma chimed in, her voice filled with enthusiasm. "And by studying these examples, we can identify best practices and strategies that we can apply to our own journey of integration," she added.

As the meeting drew to a close, Lisa left them with a challenge: "Let's use these case studies as inspiration as we continue our journey of integration. Together, we can achieve the same level of success and drive InnovateTech to new heights of growth and innovation."

With those words ringing in their ears, Emma, David, and the rest of the team left the conference room feeling inspired and invigorated. They knew that by studying the successes of others and applying those lessons to their own journey, they could achieve anything. Together, they would drive growth and propel InnovateTech into a future filled with limitless possibilities.

2

Chapter 2: Building a Strong Foundation

Establishing Core Values and Vision

In the heart of InnovateTech's headquarters, Emma, David, and the rest of the leadership team gathered in a spacious conference room, ready to embark on the crucial task of establishing core values and a shared vision for the company's future.

As they settled into their seats, Lisa, the CEO, stood at the head of the table, her presence commanding attention. With a warm smile, she began, "Thank you all for being here. Today, we're laying the groundwork for our journey of integration by defining the core values and vision that will guide us forward."

Emma felt a surge of excitement as she glanced around the room, eager to contribute to this pivotal moment in InnovateTech's history. She knew that establishing a strong foundation was essential for success, and she was ready to roll up her sleeves and get to work.

Lisa turned to a large whiteboard at the front of the room, picking up a marker with purpose. "Let's start by brainstorming our core values," she said. "What principles do we want to embody as a company?"

One by one, the team members began to call out ideas, their voices blending together in a symphony of collaboration and creativity. Integrity. Innovation. Customer-centricity. These were just a few of the values that emerged from the brainstorming session, each one reflecting the essence of what made InnovateTech unique.

As they continued to flesh out their core values, David spoke up, his voice firm with conviction. "In addition to our core values, I believe it's essential for us to define a clear vision for the future—a North Star that guides our actions and decisions."

Emma nodded in agreement, feeling a sense of alignment with David's sentiment. "Absolutely," she said. "Our vision should inspire us and unite us in pursuit of a common goal."

With that, they set to work defining their vision for the future—a vision of innovation, collaboration, and growth that would propel InnovateTech to new heights of success.

As the meeting drew to a close, Lisa stepped back to survey the whiteboard, a sense of pride evident in her eyes. "I'm incredibly proud of what we've accomplished today," she said. "By establishing our core values and vision, we've laid a solid foundation for our journey of integration. Together, we will achieve great things."

With those words ringing in their ears, Emma, David, and the rest of the team left the conference room feeling inspired and energized. They knew that by embodying their core values and working toward a shared vision, they could overcome any obstacle that stood in their way. Together, they would build a future filled with endless possibilities for InnovateTech.

Defining Roles and Responsibilities

With the core values and vision firmly established, the atmosphere in the conference room shifted as the discussion turned to defining roles and responsibilities within the company. Emma, David, and the rest of the leadership team gathered around the table, their faces illuminated by the soft glow of the overhead lights.

Lisa, the CEO, took charge of the conversation, her tone calm yet authoritative. "Now that we've established our core values and vision, it's time to ensure that everyone understands their role in bringing that vision to life," she began.

David nodded in agreement, his expression serious. "Agreed," he said. "Clarifying roles and responsibilities will help us avoid confusion and duplication of effort, allowing us to work more efficiently and effectively as a team."

Emma chimed in, her voice eager. "Exactly," she said. "By clearly defining each person's role, we can leverage their unique skills and expertise to drive toward our shared goals."

With that, they set to work mapping out the various roles and responsibilities within the company, from sales and marketing to product development and customer support. Each team member contributed their insights and perspectives, resulting in a comprehensive understanding of who was responsible for what.

As they worked through the process, tensions occasionally

flared as differences of opinion arose. But through open dialogue and respectful communication, they were able to reach consensus on each role and responsibility, ensuring that everyone felt heard and valued.

By the end of the meeting, they had produced a detailed chart outlining each team member's role, responsibilities, and areas of accountability. As they surveyed the chart, a sense of satisfaction washed over them, knowing that they had laid a solid foundation for their journey of integration.

With roles and responsibilities clearly defined, Emma, David, and the rest of the team left the conference room feeling empowered and ready to take on the challenges that lay ahead. They knew that by working together and leveraging each other's strengths, they could achieve anything. Together, they would build a future filled with endless possibilities for InnovateTech.

Setting Clear Objectives and KPIs

As the discussion in the conference room continued, the focus shifted to setting clear objectives and key performance indicators (KPIs) for the company. Emma, David, and the rest of the leadership team leaned forward, their attention fully engaged as Lisa, the CEO, began to speak.

"Having a clear set of objectives and KPIs is essential for guiding our efforts and measuring our progress," Lisa began, her voice steady and determined. "It's not enough to simply have a vision—we need to break that vision down into actionable goals that we can work toward every day."

David nodded in agreement, his eyes shining with enthusiasm. "Absolutely," he said. "By setting clear objectives and

KPIs, we can ensure that everyone is aligned and focused on achieving our shared goals."

Emma chimed in, her voice filled with determination. "And by measuring our progress against these KPIs, we can identify areas where we need to improve and make data-driven decisions to drive our success."

With that, they set to work defining their objectives and KPIs, drawing on the core values and vision they had established earlier in the meeting. Each team member contributed their ideas and insights, resulting in a comprehensive list of goals and metrics that would guide their efforts moving forward.

As they worked through the process, tensions occasionally flared as they debated the merits of different objectives and KPIs. But through open dialogue and collaboration, they were able to reach consensus on a set of clear and actionable goals.

By the end of the meeting, they had produced a detailed list of objectives and KPIs, ranging from revenue targets and customer acquisition metrics to employee satisfaction scores and product development milestones. As they reviewed the list, a sense of excitement washed over them, knowing that they now had a roadmap to guide their journey of integration.

With objectives and KPIs in place, Emma, David, and the rest of the team left the conference room feeling empowered and motivated. They knew that by working together and holding themselves accountable to these goals, they could achieve anything. Together, they would drive growth and propel InnovateTech to new heights of success.

Developing a Collaborative Culture

In the heart of InnovateTech's headquarters, the leadership team gathered once again, this time to focus on fostering a collaborative culture within the company. The atmosphere in the conference room was charged with anticipation as Emma, David, and the others took their seats, ready to delve into this crucial aspect of their journey of integration.

Lisa, the CEO, stood at the front of the room, her presence commanding attention. "Building a collaborative culture is essential for our success," she began, her voice filled with conviction. "We need to create an environment where everyone feels valued and empowered to contribute their ideas and insights."

David nodded in agreement, his expression serious. "Absolutely," he said. "By fostering collaboration and teamwork, we can leverage the collective intelligence of our team to solve problems and drive innovation."

Emma chimed in, her voice eager. "And by encouraging open communication and transparency, we can build trust and strengthen our relationships with one another," she added.

With that, they set to work brainstorming ideas for how to foster a collaborative culture within the company. From team-building activities and cross-departmental projects to open-door policies and regular feedback sessions, they explored a variety of strategies for breaking down silos and fostering collaboration.

As they discussed, tensions occasionally flared as differences of opinion arose. But through respectful dialogue and a shared commitment to their vision, they were able to find common ground and forge a path forward.

By the end of the meeting, they had produced a comprehensive plan for developing a collaborative culture within InnovateTech. From top-down leadership support to grassroots initiatives led by employees themselves, they had identified a variety of strategies for fostering collaboration and teamwork at every level of the organization.

As they surveyed the plan, a sense of excitement washed over them, knowing that they were laying the groundwork for a culture of collaboration and innovation that would drive InnovateTech to new heights of success.

With a renewed sense of purpose and determination, Emma, David, and the rest of the team left the conference room feeling inspired and ready to put their plan into action. They knew that by working together and embracing a collaborative culture, they could achieve anything. Together, they would build a future filled with endless possibilities for InnovateTech.

Training and Skill Development

The energy in the conference room was palpable as InnovateTech's leadership team gathered once more, this time to discuss the crucial topic of training and skill development. Emma, David, and their colleagues sat eagerly around the table, ready to dive into the details of how they could empower their team members with the knowledge and skills needed to drive the company's growth.

Lisa, the CEO, stood at the head of the table, her eyes shining with enthusiasm. "Our success depends not only on our strategy and vision but also on the capabilities of our people," she began. "We need to invest in training and skill development to ensure that everyone is equipped to contribute to our goals."

Emma nodded, feeling a surge of excitement. "I couldn't agree more," she said. "By providing ongoing training and development opportunities, we can help our team members grow and thrive in their roles."

David leaned forward, his expression thoughtful. "And by focusing on both hard and soft skills, we can create a well-rounded team that is adaptable and capable of overcoming any challenge," he added.

With that, they set to work outlining a comprehensive training and development program for InnovateTech. They discussed a variety of initiatives, from technical workshops and certification programs to leadership training and mentoring opportunities.

As they brainstormed, Lisa emphasized the importance of tailoring the training programs to meet the unique needs and aspirations of each team member. "We need to create personalized development plans that align with our employees' career goals and our company's objectives," she said.

Emma and David nodded in agreement, their minds racing with possibilities. They envisioned a future where InnovateTech's employees were not only highly skilled but also deeply engaged and motivated to contribute to the company's success.

By the end of the meeting, they had produced a detailed plan for implementing their training and development program. It included regular assessments to identify skill gaps, a calendar of training sessions, and a mentorship program to foster continuous learning and growth.

As they reviewed the plan, a sense of satisfaction washed over them, knowing that they were taking concrete steps to empower their team and drive InnovateTech's growth.

With training and skill development initiatives in place, Emma, David, and the rest of the team left the conference room feeling invigorated and ready to put their plan into action. They knew that by investing in their people, they could achieve anything. Together, they would build a future filled with endless possibilities for InnovateTech, driven by a team of talented and motivated individuals.

Utilizing Technology and Tools

The air buzzed with anticipation as InnovateTech's leadership team gathered for their final meeting of the day. Emma, David, and their colleagues were eager to discuss the integration of technology and tools to enhance their operations and drive their vision forward.

Lisa, the CEO, stood before them, a sense of purpose in her eyes. "Technology is a key enabler of our success," she began. "By leveraging the right tools, we can streamline our processes, improve communication, and make data-driven decisions that propel us forward."

David, ever the tech enthusiast, nodded enthusiastically. "Absolutely," he said. "We need to identify the tools that will best support our goals and ensure that everyone is trained to use them effectively."

Emma chimed in, her voice filled with determination. "And by integrating these tools across departments, we can break down silos and foster a more collaborative and efficient work environment," she added.

With that, they set to work identifying the key technologies and tools that would support their journey of integration.

They discussed a variety of options, from customer relationship management (CRM) systems and marketing automation platforms to project management software and data analytics tools.

As they delved into the details, Lisa emphasized the importance of selecting tools that were not only powerful but also user-friendly. "We need to ensure that our team members can easily adopt and utilize these tools," she said. "The goal is to enhance their productivity, not create additional complexity."

David suggested implementing a phased rollout to ensure a smooth transition and allow for any necessary adjustments. "By introducing new tools gradually, we can provide adequate training and support, and address any issues that arise," he explained.

Emma agreed, her mind racing with possibilities. She envisioned a future where InnovateTech's employees were empowered by state-of-the-art technology, seamlessly collaborating and making data-driven decisions that drove the company's success.

By the end of the meeting, they had outlined a comprehensive plan for integrating new technologies and tools into their operations. The plan included detailed timelines, training sessions, and support resources to ensure a smooth implementation.

As they reviewed the plan, a sense of excitement washed over them, knowing that they were taking concrete steps to harness the power of technology and drive InnovateTech's growth.

With the roadmap in place, Emma, David, and the rest of the team left the conference room feeling inspired and ready to put their plan into action. They knew that by leveraging the right technology and tools, they could achieve anything. Together, they would build a future filled with endless possibilities for InnovateTech, driven by innovation, collaboration, and cutting-edge technology.

3

Chapter 3: Identifying Your Target Audience

Market Research Techniques

The meeting room was alive with a sense of curiosity and determination as InnovateTech's leadership team gathered once again, this time to delve into the intricacies of identifying their target audience. Emma, David, and their colleagues were seated around the table, ready to explore the essential market research techniques that would guide their efforts.

Lisa, the CEO, stood at the head of the table, a stack of reports and charts laid out before her. She began with a confident smile, "Understanding our target audience is the cornerstone of our success. Today, we're going to explore various market research techniques that will help us gather the insights we need to connect with our customers effectively."

David leaned forward, his eyes gleaming with interest. "Market research is the foundation upon which we can build our strategies," he said. "It's about listening to our customers, understanding their needs, and using that knowledge to drive our decisions."

Emma nodded in agreement, eager to dive into the details. "By employing the right research techniques, we can uncover valuable insights that will inform our marketing and sales efforts," she added.

Lisa clicked her remote, and the projector screen came to life with a series of slides outlining different market research methods. "Let's start with surveys," she began. "Surveys are a powerful tool for gathering quantitative data from a large audience. We can use online platforms to distribute them widely and analyze the results to identify trends and preferences."

Emma raised her hand, her mind already racing with ideas. "We could design surveys that ask about customer satisfaction, product features, and future needs," she suggested. "This will help us understand what our customers value most."

Next, Lisa highlighted focus groups. "Focus groups allow us to dive deeper into qualitative insights," she explained. "By bringing together small groups of customers, we can engage in discussions that reveal their thoughts, feelings, and motivations."

David leaned back in his chair, contemplating the potential. "Focus groups could be particularly useful for exploring new product ideas or getting feedback on our marketing messages," he said. "We can gain a lot from those in-depth conversations."

As the discussion continued, Lisa introduced other techniques such as social media monitoring, competitor analysis, and customer interviews. Each method brought its own set of benefits, and the team eagerly explored how they could integrate these techniques into their research strategy.

Emma, always the strategist, emphasized the importance of combining multiple methods to get a comprehensive view. "By triangulating data from different sources, we can build a more accurate and nuanced understanding of our audience," she pointed out.

By the end of the meeting, they had developed a robust plan for conducting market research. It included detailed steps for designing surveys, organizing focus groups, and leveraging social media and competitor insights.

As they reviewed their plan, a sense of satisfaction and excitement filled the room. They knew that by employing these market research techniques, they could uncover the insights needed to identify and connect with their target audience.

With a clear roadmap in place, Emma, David, and the rest of the team left the conference room feeling empowered and ready to embark on their market research journey. They understood that by listening to their customers and leveraging data-driven insights, they could achieve anything. Together, they would build a future filled with endless possibilities for InnovateTech, driven by a deep understanding of their audience and a commitment to meeting their needs.

Creating Buyer Personas

The meeting room buzzed with energy as InnovateTech's leadership team reconvened to take their market research findings and translate them into actionable strategies. Emma, David, and their colleagues were excited to dive into the process of creating buyer personas—fictional representations of their ideal customers based on real data.

Lisa, the CEO, began the session with a sense of purpose. "Now that we've gathered our market research data, it's time to bring it to life by creating buyer personas," she said. "These personas will help us understand our customers on a deeper level and tailor our strategies to meet their needs."

Emma leaned forward, her eyes bright with anticipation. "Buyer personas will allow us to humanize our audience and ensure that our marketing and sales efforts resonate with the people we're trying to reach," she added.

David nodded in agreement, flipping open his notebook. "Let's start by identifying the key segments within our target audience," he suggested. "We can use the data from our surveys, focus groups, and social media monitoring to define these segments."

Lisa clicked her remote, and the projector displayed a blank template for a buyer persona. "Let's create our first persona together," she said, gesturing to the screen. "We'll start with a segment that emerged strongly in our research: tech-savvy young professionals."

The team began brainstorming, drawing from the rich data they had collected. "Let's name her 'Techie Tina,'" David suggested, eliciting nods and smiles from around the table.

"Techie Tina is in her late twenties," Emma said, her voice thoughtful. "She works in a fast-paced tech environment and values innovation and efficiency."

Lisa added more details to the template. "She's highly educated, with a background in computer science. She's always looking for the latest tools and software to streamline her work."

David chimed in, "Based on our survey data, we know that

Tina spends a lot of time on tech forums and social media platforms like LinkedIn and Twitter. She's influenced by thought leaders in the tech industry."

As they continued to flesh out Techie Tina's persona, they discussed her goals, challenges, and preferred communication channels. They identified that she valued seamless user experiences and was willing to pay a premium for high-quality, reliable products.

"Understanding Tina's pain points is crucial," Emma noted. "She struggles with finding products that integrate well with her existing tools and often feels overwhelmed by the sheer number of options available."

With Techie Tina's persona complete, Lisa prompted the team to move on to another key segment: small business owners. They named this persona "Entrepreneur Eric."

"Eric is in his mid-forties," David began. "He owns a small but growing business and is looking for scalable solutions that can help him manage his operations more efficiently."

Emma added, "Eric is cost-conscious but willing to invest in solutions that offer a clear return on investment. He values customer support and needs a product that is easy to implement and use."

The team continued to build out Entrepreneur Eric's persona, detailing his background, needs, and behaviors. They discussed how Eric relied on word-of-mouth recommendations and industry publications to make purchasing decisions.

By the end of the session, they had created detailed personas for Techie Tina, Entrepreneur Eric, and several other key segments. These personas provided a vivid picture of their target audience, grounded in real data and enriched with human details.

As they reviewed the personas, a sense of accomplishment filled the room. They knew that these buyer personas would serve as a valuable tool, guiding their marketing, sales, and product development efforts.

With buyer personas in hand, Emma, David, and the rest of the team left the conference room feeling confident and inspired. They understood that by putting a face to their data, they could connect with their audience on a deeper level and create strategies that truly resonated. Together, they would build a future filled with endless possibilities for InnovateTech, driven by a deep understanding of their customers and a commitment to meeting their needs.

Segmenting Your Market

The room was charged with anticipation as InnovateTech's leadership team gathered to tackle the next step in their market research journey: segmenting their market. Emma, David, and their colleagues sat at the table, ready to transform the buyer personas they had created into actionable segments that would guide their marketing and sales strategies.

Lisa, the CEO, opened the meeting with a confident smile. "Now that we've created our buyer personas, it's time to segment our market," she began. "By dividing our audience into distinct groups, we can tailor our strategies to meet the specific needs and preferences of each segment."

David leaned forward, his eyes gleaming with excitement. "Segmentation allows us to be more precise and effective in our marketing efforts," he said. "It's about understanding the unique characteristics of each group and delivering targeted messages that resonate with them."

Emma nodded, eager to dive in. "Let's start by identifying the key criteria for segmenting our market," she suggested. "We can use demographic, geographic, psychographic, and behavioral factors to define our segments."

Lisa clicked her remote, and the projector displayed a list of segmentation criteria. "First, let's look at demographic factors," she said. "Age, gender, income, education level, and occupation can all help us define our segments."

The team began brainstorming, drawing from the rich data they had collected. They identified several demographic segments, including young professionals, middle-aged small business owners, and retirees looking for tech solutions to stay connected.

Next, they moved on to geographic segmentation. "We need to consider where our customers are located," David said. "Urban areas, suburban neighborhoods, and rural regions all have different needs and preferences."

Emma added, "We can also segment based on regional factors, such as climate and cultural differences. This will help us tailor our messaging to resonate with customers in different parts of the country."

With geographic segments defined, they turned to psychographic factors. "This is about understanding our customers' lifestyles, values, and interests," Lisa explained. "For example, Techie Tina values innovation and efficiency, while Entrepreneur Eric is focused on scalability and customer support."

David chimed in, "We can also segment based on attitudes and behaviors. Some customers may be early adopters of new technology, while others may be more cautious and prefer proven solutions."

As they continued to discuss, the team created a matrix that combined these various criteria, resulting in a series of well-defined market segments. They identified segments such as tech-savvy millennials in urban areas, cost-conscious small business owners in suburban neighborhoods, and retirees in rural regions seeking reliable tech solutions.

By the end of the session, they had developed a comprehensive segmentation strategy that provided a clear roadmap for targeting their audience. Each segment was detailed, with specific characteristics, needs, and preferences outlined.

As they reviewed their segmentation plan, a sense of satisfaction and excitement filled the room. They knew that by segmenting their market, they could deliver more personalized and effective marketing messages, ultimately driving better results.

With their market segments clearly defined, Emma, David, and the rest of the team left the conference room feeling inspired and ready to put their plan into action. They understood that by tailoring their strategies to meet the unique needs of each segment, they could connect with their audience on a deeper level and achieve greater success. Together, they would build a future filled with endless possibilities for InnovateTech, driven by a nuanced understanding of their market and a commitment to meeting their customers' needs.

Analyzing Customer Data

As the sun dipped below the horizon, casting a warm glow through the large windows of InnovateTech's meeting room, the leadership team gathered once more. This time, their focus was on the critical task of analyzing customer data. Emma,

David, and their colleagues sat with laptops open, ready to dive into the data that would reveal deeper insights about their market segments.

Lisa, the CEO, stood at the head of the table, a sense of purpose in her voice. "Now that we've segmented our market, it's time to analyze the customer data we've collected," she began. "This will help us understand the behaviors, preferences, and pain points of each segment in greater detail."

David, ever the data enthusiast, nodded eagerly. "Customer data is a goldmine of information," he said. "By analyzing it, we can uncover patterns and trends that will guide our marketing and sales strategies."

Emma leaned forward, her eyes filled with determination. "Let's start by looking at our CRM and sales data," she suggested. "We can analyze purchase history, customer interactions, and feedback to identify key trends and preferences."

Lisa clicked her remote, and the projector displayed a dashboard filled with charts and graphs. "Here's an overview of our current data," she said. "Let's drill down into each segment and see what insights we can uncover."

The team began by examining the data for Techie Tina, their tech-savvy young professional persona. They analyzed her purchase history, noting that she frequently bought cutting-edge gadgets and software subscriptions. They also looked at her interaction history, observing that she preferred engaging with the company through social media and online chat.

"Techie Tina values efficiency and innovation," David noted. "She responds well to new product announcements and appreciates quick, responsive customer support."

Next, they turned their attention to Entrepreneur Eric, the small business owner. The data revealed that Eric often purchased scalable solutions and valued customer support highly. His feedback indicated a need for more streamlined onboarding processes and ongoing training resources.

"Eric is focused on growth and efficiency," Emma observed. "He needs solutions that can grow with his business and reliable support to help him get the most out of our products."

As they continued to analyze the data for their other segments, they identified common themes and unique challenges for each group. They looked at usage patterns, engagement metrics, and customer satisfaction scores, building a detailed picture of their audience's needs and behaviors.

Lisa emphasized the importance of turning these insights into actionable strategies. "We need to use this data to tailor our marketing messages, improve our products, and enhance our customer support," she said.

David suggested creating targeted campaigns based on the insights they had gathered. "We can develop personalized email campaigns, social media content, and promotional offers for each segment," he said. "By addressing their specific needs and preferences, we'll be more effective in reaching and engaging our customers."

Emma agreed, her mind racing with possibilities. "We should also use this data to inform our product development and customer service strategies," she added. "By understanding what our customers want and need, we can continuously improve and innovate."

By the end of the meeting, they had developed a comprehensive plan for leveraging their customer data. It included detailed steps for analyzing ongoing data, creating targeted marketing campaigns, and using insights to drive product development and customer service improvements.

As they reviewed their plan, a sense of accomplishment and excitement filled the room. They knew that by harnessing the power of customer data, they could make more informed decisions and drive greater success.

With a clear roadmap in place, Emma, David, and the rest of the team left the conference room feeling inspired and ready to put their plan into action. They understood that by analyzing customer data and using it to inform their strategies, they could achieve anything. Together, they would build a future filled with endless possibilities for InnovateTech, driven by data-driven insights and a commitment to meeting their customers' needs.

Understanding Customer Pain Points

The atmosphere in InnovateTech's meeting room was one of deep focus and determination. The leadership team, comprising Emma, David, and their colleagues, had gathered to delve into a crucial aspect of their market research journey: understanding customer pain points. This step would allow them to empathize with their customers' challenges and tailor solutions that truly addressed their needs.

Lisa, the CEO, began the session with a sense of urgency. "Identifying and understanding our customers' pain points is critical," she said. "It's not enough to know who they are—we need to understand their struggles and frustrations to provide real value."

David leaned forward, his eyes sharp with concentration. "Pain points are the problems our customers face that we can solve," he said. "By addressing these issues, we can build stronger relationships and enhance customer loyalty."

CHAPTER 3: IDENTIFYING YOUR TARGET AUDIENCE

Emma, eager to dive into the details, suggested starting with the data they had previously analyzed. "Let's look at the feedback and customer interactions we've gathered," she said. "This data can help us pinpoint specific challenges our customers are facing."

Lisa clicked her remote, and the projector displayed a series of customer feedback excerpts and interaction logs. "Let's start with Techie Tina," she said. "What pain points does she encounter?"

The team began examining the data, noting several recurring themes. Techie Tina often expressed frustration with the lack of integration between different software tools. She also highlighted the difficulty in keeping up with rapid technological changes and finding reliable, user-friendly products.

"Integration is a major pain point for Tina," David observed. "She needs tools that work seamlessly together and help her stay efficient."

Emma added, "She also struggles with the pace of technological change. She needs solutions that are easy to adopt and keep her ahead of the curve without overwhelming her."

Next, they turned to Entrepreneur Eric. His feedback revealed issues with the complexity of onboarding new technology and the challenge of finding scalable solutions that could grow with his business. He also mentioned the importance of reliable customer support and training resources.

"Eric needs a smooth onboarding process," Emma noted. "He wants to quickly integrate new technology without disrupting his operations."

David agreed, adding, "And scalability is crucial for him. He needs solutions that can grow with his business, along with consistent support and training."

As they continued to analyze feedback from other segments, they identified common pain points such as the need for better customer service, more intuitive user interfaces, and clearer communication about product updates and features.

Lisa emphasized the importance of addressing these pain points in their strategies. "By solving these problems, we can differentiate ourselves from competitors and build stronger customer relationships," she said.

David suggested incorporating these insights into their product development and customer service processes. "We should prioritize features that enhance integration, simplify onboarding, and offer scalability," he said. "And we need to ensure our customer support is proactive and responsive."

Emma agreed, her mind racing with ideas. "We can also create educational content and resources to help our customers navigate technological changes and maximize their use of our products," she added.

By the end of the meeting, they had developed a comprehensive plan to address their customers' pain points. It included specific actions for product development, customer support, and marketing strategies designed to alleviate their customers' challenges and enhance their experience.

As they reviewed their plan, a sense of purpose and excitement filled the room. They knew that by understanding and addressing their customers' pain points, they could create meaningful solutions and build lasting relationships.

With a clear roadmap in place, Emma, David, and the rest of the team left the conference room feeling empowered and ready to put their plan into action. They understood that by empathizing with their customers and solving their problems, they could achieve anything. Together, they would build a future filled with endless possibilities for InnovateTech, driven by a deep understanding of their customers' pain points and a commitment to delivering real value.

Tailoring Your Message

The room buzzed with renewed energy as InnovateTech's leadership team gathered once more. Emma, David, and their colleagues were ready to discuss the final, crucial step of their market research journey: tailoring their message to address the unique needs and pain points of their identified market segments.

Lisa, the CEO, opened the meeting with a sense of enthusiasm. "Now that we understand our customers' pain points, it's time to tailor our messages to address these specific needs," she began. "This is how we connect with our audience on a deeper level and show them that we truly understand and care about their challenges."

David leaned forward, excitement in his voice. "Personalization is key," he said. "We need to speak directly to our customers' concerns and demonstrate how our solutions can help them."

Emma, ever the strategist, suggested starting with their buyer personas. "Let's use Techie Tina and Entrepreneur Eric as examples," she said. "How can we craft messages that resonate with their unique challenges and aspirations?"

Lisa clicked her remote, and the projector displayed a blank messaging framework. "For Techie Tina," she began, "we need to emphasize innovation and efficiency. Our message should highlight how our products integrate seamlessly with her existing tools and keep her ahead of technological changes."

David chimed in, "We could use a tagline like, 'Stay ahead of the curve with seamless integration and cutting-edge technology.' We should also highlight specific features that save time and improve productivity."

Emma nodded, adding, "And we can create content that addresses her pain points, like blog posts on the benefits of integration, case studies showcasing successful implementations, and social media updates about new features and updates."

Next, they turned their attention to Entrepreneur Eric. "Eric values scalability and reliable support," Lisa said. "Our message should focus on how our solutions can grow with his business and provide the support he needs to succeed."

David suggested a tagline, "Empower your growth with scalable solutions and unmatched support." He continued, "We should highlight our dedicated customer service, easy onboarding process, and training resources in our messaging."

Emma added, "For Eric, we can create webinars on maximizing ROI, customer testimonials about business growth, and email campaigns that offer tips and resources for small business owners."

As they continued to craft tailored messages for their other segments, they focused on addressing each group's specific pain points and aspirations. They discussed the importance of using the right channels to reach their audience, whether through social media, email, blogs, or direct sales.

Lisa emphasized the need for consistency across all communication channels. "Our messaging should be unified and consistent, no matter where our customers encounter it," she said. "This builds trust and reinforces our commitment to solving their problems."

David suggested leveraging technology to personalize their communication further. "We can use marketing automation to deliver tailored content based on customer behavior and preferences," he said. "This ensures that our messages are relevant and timely."

By the end of the meeting, they had developed a comprehensive messaging strategy for each of their key segments. Each message was carefully crafted to address the specific needs and challenges of their audience, with clear value propositions and calls to action.

As they reviewed their messaging frameworks, a sense of accomplishment and excitement filled the room. They knew that by tailoring their messages, they could connect with their customers on a deeper level and drive greater engagement and loyalty.

With a clear plan in place, Emma, David, and the rest of the team left the conference room feeling inspired and ready to implement their tailored messaging strategy. They understood that by speaking directly to their customers' needs and demonstrating genuine empathy and understanding, they could achieve anything. Together, they would build a future filled with endless possibilities for InnovateTech, driven by personalized communication and a commitment to delivering real value.

4

Chapter 4: Crafting Your Brand Story

Defining Your Brand Identity

The conference room was bathed in the morning light, casting a hopeful glow over InnovateTech's leadership team as they gathered to embark on a new phase of their journey: crafting their brand story. Emma, David, and their colleagues were eager to dive into the process of defining their brand identity, the very essence that would shape their narrative and resonate with their audience.

Lisa, the CEO, stood at the head of the table, a sense of excitement in her voice. "Today, we begin crafting our brand story," she said. "Our brand identity is the foundation of this story. It's who we are, what we stand for, and how we want to be perceived."

David leaned forward, his eyes gleaming with anticipation. "Our brand identity needs to reflect our core values and vision," he said. "It should be authentic and resonate with our customers."

CHAPTER 4: CRAFTING YOUR BRAND STORY

Emma, always the strategist, suggested starting with a brainstorming session. "Let's identify the key elements of our brand identity," she said. "We need to define our mission, vision, values, and unique selling propositions."

Lisa clicked her remote, and the projector displayed a blank framework for defining brand identity. "First, let's articulate our mission," she began. "What is our purpose? Why do we exist?"

The room fell silent as everyone pondered this fundamental question. After a moment, Emma spoke up. "Our mission is to empower individuals and businesses through innovative technology solutions that enhance efficiency and drive growth."

David nodded in agreement. "Our vision should be to become a leading provider of integrated tech solutions, known for our commitment to innovation, quality, and customer support."

As they continued to discuss, they identified core values that would guide their brand. "Innovation, integrity, customer-centricity, and collaboration," Lisa said, jotting down the words. "These values should permeate everything we do."

Next, they turned to their unique selling propositions (USPs). "What sets us apart from our competitors?" David asked. "Why should customers choose us?"

Emma leaned forward, her voice confident. "Our seamless integration capabilities, exceptional customer support, and commitment to staying ahead of technological trends are our key differentiators."

With the foundational elements of their brand identity defined, the team began to discuss how these elements would shape their brand story. Lisa emphasized the importance of consistency. "Our brand story should be consistent across all touchpoints," she said. "From our website to our social media to our customer interactions, the message should be unified."

David suggested creating a brand manifesto that encapsulated their identity. "A manifesto can serve as a guiding document," he said. "It will help ensure that everyone in the company understands and embodies our brand."

Emma proposed bringing their brand story to life through visuals and storytelling. "Our logo, color palette, and design elements should reflect our identity," she said. "And our marketing content should tell a compelling story that resonates with our audience."

By the end of the meeting, they had crafted a clear and compelling brand identity. It encapsulated their mission, vision, values, and unique selling propositions, providing a strong foundation for their brand story.

As they reviewed their work, a sense of pride and excitement filled the room. They knew that by defining their brand identity, they had taken a crucial step toward building a powerful and resonant brand story.

With a clear identity in place, Emma, David, and the rest of the team left the conference room feeling inspired and ready to bring their brand story to life. They understood that by staying true to their identity and communicating it consistently, they could create a brand that connected deeply with their customers. Together, they would build a future filled with endless possibilities for InnovateTech, driven by a strong brand identity and a commitment to excellence.

Creating a Compelling Narrative

The energy in InnovateTech's conference room was palpable as the leadership team reconvened. Having defined their brand identity, they were now ready to weave these elements into a compelling narrative that would captivate their audience and set them apart in the market. Emma, David, and their colleagues settled in, ready to transform their identity into a story that resonated with emotion and purpose.

Lisa, the CEO, began the session with a sense of enthusiasm. "Now that we have a clear brand identity, it's time to create our brand narrative," she said. "This narrative will be the story we tell our customers, partners, and the world. It needs to be compelling, authentic, and inspiring."

David leaned forward, his eyes sparkling with excitement. "A great narrative connects with people on an emotional level," he said. "It's about more than just what we do—it's about why we do it and the impact we want to make."

Emma, always the strategist, suggested starting with the core elements of their narrative. "We need to identify the key themes and messages that will form the backbone of our story," she said. "Let's think about our origin, our journey, and our vision for the future."

Lisa clicked her remote, and the projector displayed a blank story framework. "Let's begin with our origin," she said. "How did InnovateTech start? What inspired our founders to create this company?"

The room fell silent as everyone reflected on the company's beginnings. After a moment, Emma spoke up. "InnovateTech was born out of a desire to bridge the gap between complex technology and everyday users," she said. "Our founders saw the frustration people faced with disjointed, hard-to-use tech solutions and wanted to create something different—something seamless and user-friendly."

David added, "They believed that technology should empower people, not overwhelm them. This vision of empowerment through innovation has driven us from the start."

With their origin story taking shape, the team moved on to their journey. "What challenges have we overcome?" Lisa asked. "How have we grown and evolved?"

Emma leaned forward, her voice filled with passion. "We've faced numerous challenges, from rapid technological changes to fierce competition," she said. "But through it all, we've remained committed to our core values of innovation, integrity, customer-centricity, and collaboration. These values have guided us and helped us build strong relationships with our customers."

David nodded, adding, "Our journey has been one of continuous learning and adaptation. We've listened to our customers, embraced new ideas, and constantly sought to improve our products and services."

Next, they turned to their vision for the future. "What impact do we want to make?" Lisa asked. "What is our ultimate goal?"

Emma's eyes shone with determination. "We want to create a world where technology seamlessly integrates into people's lives, enhancing their productivity and enabling them to achieve their goals," she said. "Our vision is to be a leader in innovative tech solutions, known for our commitment to quality and customer satisfaction."

David suggested weaving these elements into a cohesive narrative. "Let's start with our origin and move through our journey to our vision," he said. "We should highlight the challenges we've faced, the values that guide us, and the impact we want to make."

As they crafted the narrative, they emphasized the human element of their story. They spoke of the founders' passion for technology, the team's dedication to customer success, and the stories of customers whose lives had been transformed by InnovateTech's solutions.

By the end of the session, they had created a powerful and compelling brand narrative. It was a story of vision, perseverance, and impact—one that resonated with the heart and soul of InnovateTech.

As they reviewed their narrative, a sense of pride and excitement filled the room. They knew that this story would connect with their audience on a deep level, inspiring trust and loyalty.

With their brand narrative complete, Emma, David, and the rest of the team left the conference room feeling inspired and ready to share their story with the world. They understood that by telling a compelling and authentic story, they could create a powerful connection with their customers and build a lasting brand. Together, they would build a future filled with endless possibilities for InnovateTech, driven by a strong narrative and a commitment to making a difference.

Aligning Brand Story with Customer Values

In the hushed ambiance of the conference room, the InnovateTech team reconvened, their focus now honed on the critical task of aligning their brand story with the values of their customers. Emma, David, and their colleagues gathered around the table, poised to bridge the narrative gap between their company ethos and the aspirations of their audience.

Lisa, the CEO, set the tone with a poised demeanor. "Now that we have sculpted our brand narrative, it's imperative to ensure that it resonates with the values of our customers," she began. "Our story must strike a chord with their beliefs and aspirations."

David, his gaze determined, chimed in. "Our customers are at the heart of our story. We must weave their values seamlessly into our narrative to foster a sense of kinship and alignment."

Emma nodded in agreement. "Understanding our customers' values is paramount. It enables us to craft a narrative that not only resonates with them but also establishes a genuine connection."

Lisa gestured toward the blank canvas projected on the screen. "Let's map out the core values of our target audience and find the intersection with our brand narrative."

As they delved into the exercise, they uncovered a tapestry of shared values. Their customers valued innovation, reliability, and customer-centricity. They sought solutions that empowered them to achieve their goals while aligning with their ethical and environmental principles.

David interjected, "Our brand narrative echoes these values—we are committed to innovation, integrity, and putting the customer first. We must emphasize these shared values to forge a strong connection."

Emma nodded, her expression thoughtful. "We can illustrate how our products and services align with their values through storytelling. Highlighting customer success stories and testimonials can showcase the tangible impact of our solutions on their lives."

Lisa concurred, "Our marketing materials, website content, and social media posts should echo these shared values. By consistently communicating our alignment with their values, we build trust and loyalty."

David suggested integrating feedback mechanisms to gauge the resonance of their narrative with customers' values continuously. "Regular feedback loops allow us to refine our messaging and ensure ongoing alignment with our audience."

Emma proposed collaboration with influencers and thought leaders who embodied the values cherished by their audience. "Their endorsement can reinforce the authenticity of our narrative and amplify its reach," she said.

As they continued to brainstorm, a palpable sense of synergy filled the room. They were forging a connection between their brand story and the values of their customers, creating a tapestry of resonance and authenticity.

With their alignment strategy defined, Emma, David, and the rest of the team left the conference room invigorated and determined. They understood that by aligning their brand story with the values of their customers, they could foster a deep connection and cultivate enduring loyalty. Together, they would build a future where their narrative resonated with the hearts and minds of their audience, forging a path toward shared success.

Communicating Consistently Across Channels

In the vibrant ambiance of the conference room, InnovateTech's leadership team convened once more, their attention now turned towards the imperative task of ensuring consistent communication of their brand story across various channels. With Emma, David, and their colleagues gathered around the table, they were poised to synchronize their narrative seamlessly across every touchpoint, ensuring a unified brand experience for their audience.

Lisa, the CEO, assumed a poised stance, radiating a sense of determination. "Now that we've sculpted our brand narrative, it's essential to maintain consistency in how we communicate it across all channels," she began. "Our story must resonate harmoniously, regardless of where our audience encounters it."

David, his expression resolute, nodded in agreement. "Consistency is key to building brand trust and recognition," he remarked. "We must ensure that our narrative remains steadfast, no matter the medium through which it is conveyed."

Emma, ever the strategist, interjected with enthusiasm. "Let's establish a framework for ensuring consistent communication," she proposed. "This entails aligning our messaging, visuals, and tone across all channels—from our website and social media to our marketing materials and customer interactions."

Lisa gestured towards the blank canvas projected on the screen. "Let's map out our communication strategy," she suggested. "Starting with our key messages, we'll outline how they'll be conveyed through various channels while maintaining uniformity."

As they embarked on the task, they delineated their core messages—innovation, customer-centricity, reliability—and elucidated how each would be conveyed through diverse channels.

David highlighted, "Our website should serve as the cornerstone of our communication efforts, housing our brand story, mission, and values in a compelling and accessible manner."

Emma echoed his sentiment, "Social media platforms provide an opportunity for real-time engagement. We'll disseminate our narrative through engaging content, fostering dialogue and connection with our audience."

Lisa underscored the importance of consistency in tone and visual identity. "Whether it's an email campaign or a customer service interaction, our tone should be consistent—warm, approachable, and customer-focused," she emphasized.

David suggested leveraging automation tools to ensure consistency across digital channels. "Marketing automation enables us to deliver targeted messages to our audience, maintaining brand consistency while scaling our efforts," he remarked.

Emma proposed regular audits to evaluate the alignment of their communication efforts with their brand narrative. "By periodically reviewing our messaging and visual assets, we can identify any discrepancies and make necessary adjustments to maintain consistency," she said.

As they meticulously outlined their communication strategy, a sense of cohesion pervaded the room. They were forging a roadmap for ensuring that their brand story resonated consistently across every channel, fostering trust and loyalty with their audience.

With their communication strategy delineated, Emma, David, and the rest of the team departed the conference room with renewed purpose. They understood that by communicating their brand story consistently across all channels, they could cultivate a cohesive brand identity and forge lasting connections with their audience. Together, they would embark on a journey where every interaction echoed the heart and soul of InnovateTech's narrative, guiding their audience towards shared success.

Using Storytelling to Engage

In the cozy atmosphere of InnovateTech's conference room, the leadership team gathered once again, their focus now on harnessing the power of storytelling to captivate and engage their audience. With Emma, David, and their colleagues seated around the table, they were poised to infuse their brand narrative with the magic of storytelling, fostering a deeper connection with their audience.

Lisa, the CEO, assumed a contemplative stance, her eyes alight with anticipation. "Now that we've crafted our brand narrative, it's time to breathe life into it through the art of storytelling," she began. "Storytelling has the power to evoke emotion, spark imagination, and forge lasting connections with our audience."

David, his gaze filled with conviction, nodded in agreement. "By weaving our brand narrative into compelling stories, we can create memorable experiences that resonate with our audience on a profound level," he remarked. "It's about connecting with them on an emotional level and inspiring them to become part of our story."

Emma, ever the storyteller at heart, interjected with enthusiasm. "Let's explore different storytelling techniques and mediums to bring our brand narrative to life," she suggested. "From video testimonials and customer success stories to blog posts and social media campaigns, there are endless opportunities to engage our audience through storytelling."

CHAPTER 4: CRAFTING YOUR BRAND STORY

Lisa gestured towards the blank canvas projected on the screen. "Let's map out our storytelling strategy," she proposed. "Starting with our key messages, we'll outline how they'll be conveyed through compelling narratives across various mediums."

As they embarked on the task, they discussed the power of storytelling to humanize their brand and make it relatable to their audience.

David highlighted, "Customer success stories serve as powerful testimonials to the impact of our solutions. By sharing real-life experiences, we can demonstrate the tangible benefits of choosing InnovateTech."

Emma echoed his sentiment, "Behind-the-scenes stories offer a glimpse into the people and processes behind our products and services. They humanize our brand and foster a sense of connection with our audience."

Lisa emphasized the importance of authenticity in storytelling. "Our stories should be genuine and relatable, reflecting the values and experiences of our audience," she remarked. "By sharing stories that resonate with their lives, we can forge deeper connections and inspire loyalty."

David suggested leveraging user-generated content to amplify their storytelling efforts. "Encouraging our customers to share their stories and experiences with our brand allows us to tap into the power of social proof and word-of-mouth marketing," he remarked.

Emma proposed integrating storytelling into every aspect of their communication strategy. "From website content and email campaigns to social media posts and customer interactions, storytelling should permeate every touchpoint," she said. "It's about creating a cohesive narrative that resonates with our audience across every channel."

As they meticulously outlined their storytelling strategy, a sense of excitement filled the room. They were embarking on a journey to infuse their brand narrative with the power of storytelling, creating experiences that would captivate and inspire their audience.

With their storytelling strategy delineated, Emma, David, and the rest of the team departed the conference room with renewed energy and purpose. They understood that by harnessing the power of storytelling, they could create meaningful connections with their audience and bring their brand narrative to life in a way that resonated deeply. Together, they would embark on a storytelling journey where every tale echoed the essence of InnovateTech's narrative, guiding their audience towards shared success.

Measuring Brand Impact

As the sunlight streamed through the windows of InnovateTech's conference room, illuminating the faces of the leadership team, they gathered once more with a sense of purpose. With Emma, David, and their colleagues seated around the table, their focus shifted to the crucial task of measuring the impact of their brand narrative. They were poised to evaluate how effectively their storytelling efforts resonated with their audience and drove tangible results.

Lisa, the CEO, assumed a thoughtful demeanor, her gaze scanning the room with intent. "Now that we've woven our brand narrative into compelling stories, it's imperative to measure the impact of our efforts," she began. "We need to understand how effectively our storytelling resonates with

CHAPTER 4: CRAFTING YOUR BRAND STORY

our audience and contributes to our overarching business goals."

David, his expression analytical, nodded in agreement. "By establishing key performance indicators (KPIs) and tracking metrics, we can gauge the effectiveness of our storytelling efforts and identify areas for improvement," he remarked. "It's about quantifying the impact of our brand narrative in driving engagement, loyalty, and ultimately, business growth."

Emma, ever the strategist, interjected with enthusiasm. "Let's define our KPIs and establish a framework for measuring brand impact," she suggested. "From website traffic and social media engagement to customer feedback and sales conversions, there are myriad metrics we can track to assess the effectiveness of our storytelling."

Lisa gestured towards the blank canvas projected on the screen. "Let's map out our measurement strategy," she proposed. "Starting with our key objectives, we'll outline the KPIs and metrics that align with our business goals and provide insights into the impact of our brand narrative."

As they embarked on the task, they discussed the importance of aligning their measurement efforts with their overarching business objectives.

David highlighted, "Website traffic and engagement metrics, such as bounce rate, time on page, and conversion rate, provide insights into how effectively our brand narrative resonates with visitors and drives them to take action."

Emma echoed his sentiment, "Social media engagement metrics, such as likes, comments, shares, and follower growth, offer valuable insights into how effectively our storytelling efforts engage our audience and foster dialogue."

Lisa emphasized the importance of customer feedback and

sentiment analysis. "By soliciting feedback from our audience and analyzing sentiment across various channels, we can gain valuable insights into how our brand narrative is perceived and identify areas for improvement," she remarked.

David suggested leveraging marketing automation tools to streamline data collection and analysis. "By automating data collection and reporting processes, we can gain real-time insights into the impact of our storytelling efforts and make data-driven decisions to optimize our strategy," he remarked.

Emma proposed regular performance reviews to evaluate the effectiveness of their storytelling efforts and iterate on their strategy. "By conducting regular assessments and adjusting our approach based on performance data, we can continuously optimize our storytelling efforts to drive maximum impact," she remarked.

As they meticulously outlined their measurement strategy, a sense of clarity and purpose filled the room. They were embarking on a journey to quantify the impact of their brand narrative and ensure that their storytelling efforts drove tangible results.

With their measurement strategy delineated, Emma, David, and the rest of the team departed the conference room with renewed focus and determination. They understood that by measuring the impact of their brand narrative, they could gain valuable insights into its effectiveness and drive continuous improvement. Together, they would embark on a journey where every data point echoed the resonance of InnovateTech's narrative, guiding their audience towards shared success.

5

Chapter 5: Developing Effective Marketing Strategies

Setting Marketing Goals

The InnovateTech conference room buzzed with energy as the leadership team gathered to tackle the next phase of their journey: developing effective marketing strategies. Emma, David, Lisa, and their colleagues were ready to set clear, actionable marketing goals that would drive their initiatives and ensure they reached their target audience effectively.

Lisa, the CEO, stood at the front of the room, her eyes shining with determination. "Today, we focus on setting our marketing goals," she began. "Clear goals provide direction and help us measure our success. They are the foundation upon which we build our strategies."

David, ever the pragmatist, nodded in agreement. "Goals need to be specific, measurable, achievable, relevant, and time-bound—SMART goals," he remarked. "This ensures that we have a clear roadmap and can track our progress effectively."

Emma, always the strategist, interjected with enthusiasm. "Let's start by identifying our primary objectives," she suggested. "What do we want to achieve with our marketing efforts? Increased brand awareness, lead generation, customer retention, or perhaps all of these?"

Lisa clicked her remote, and the projector displayed a blank framework for setting marketing goals. "Let's break it down," she said. "We'll start with our overarching business objectives and align our marketing goals to support them."

As they embarked on the task, the team discussed the company's long-term vision and how marketing could play a pivotal role in achieving it.

David highlighted, "One of our primary business objectives is to increase market share. To support this, a key marketing goal could be to expand our brand presence and reach new customer segments."

Emma echoed his sentiment, "Another objective is to drive revenue growth. For marketing, this translates into generating high-quality leads that convert into loyal customers."

Lisa emphasized the importance of customer satisfaction and loyalty. "Retaining existing customers is as crucial as acquiring new ones," she remarked. "A marketing goal could be to enhance customer engagement and build stronger relationships with our current customer base."

With these objectives in mind, they began to formulate specific marketing goals.

David suggested, "For brand awareness, we could aim to increase our social media following by 25% over the next six months and boost website traffic by 30%."

Emma proposed a goal for lead generation, "Let's aim to

generate 500 new qualified leads per quarter through targeted marketing campaigns and content marketing efforts."

Lisa added a goal for customer retention, "We should strive to increase our customer retention rate by 15% within the next year through personalized marketing and improved customer support."

As they meticulously outlined their goals, a sense of clarity and focus filled the room. They were setting the foundation for their marketing strategies, ensuring that each goal was aligned with their overarching business objectives and was SMART.

David suggested setting up a tracking system to monitor their progress. "We need to establish KPIs for each goal and use analytics tools to track our performance," he remarked. "Regular reviews will help us stay on track and make data-driven adjustments as needed."

Emma proposed integrating feedback loops to continuously refine their goals and strategies. "By gathering insights from our marketing efforts and customer interactions, we can iteratively improve our approach and ensure that we're meeting our goals effectively," she said.

With their marketing goals clearly defined and a robust tracking system in place, the team felt a renewed sense of purpose. They understood that these goals would serve as their compass, guiding their marketing efforts and driving them towards success.

As they left the conference room, Emma, David, Lisa, and the rest of the team felt a surge of confidence and determination. They knew that by setting clear, actionable marketing goals, they were laying the groundwork for impactful strategies that would propel InnovateTech towards its vision. Together, they would embark on a journey where each goal echoed the promise of growth and success, guiding their audience towards shared prosperity.

Choosing the Right Channels

The InnovateTech conference room was buzzing with focused energy as the leadership team reconvened. Emma, David, Lisa, and their colleagues were ready to delve into the next crucial step of their marketing strategy: selecting the right channels to effectively reach their target audience and achieve their marketing goals.

Lisa, the CEO, stood at the front, her determination palpable. "With our marketing goals set, it's time to choose the channels through which we will communicate our message," she began. "Selecting the right channels is essential for ensuring our efforts resonate with our target audience and drive the desired results."

David, the analytical mind, nodded thoughtfully. "It's not just about being present on multiple platforms," he remarked. "It's about strategically choosing the channels that align with our audience's preferences and behaviors."

Emma, ever the strategist, chimed in with enthusiasm. "Let's start by identifying where our target audience spends their time and how they prefer to engage with content," she suggested. "We need to consider demographics, psychographics, and behavioral data to make informed decisions."

Lisa clicked her remote, and the projector displayed a matrix of potential marketing channels. "We'll evaluate each channel based on its ability to reach our target audience, align with our brand narrative, and support our marketing goals," she said.

The team embarked on a detailed discussion, considering a variety of channels and their respective strengths.

David highlighted the importance of digital channels. "Our website is our primary digital asset," he noted. "We need to ensure it's optimized for user experience and search engines. Additionally, search engine marketing (SEM) can drive targeted traffic to our site."

Emma emphasized the power of social media. "Platforms like LinkedIn, Twitter, and Instagram offer opportunities for direct engagement and community building," she said. "We can leverage these platforms to share our brand story, engage with our audience, and drive traffic to our website."

Lisa underscored the significance of email marketing. "Email remains one of the most effective channels for personalized communication," she remarked. "We can use it to nurture leads, share updates, and build strong relationships with our customers."

David suggested exploring content marketing. "Creating valuable content such as blog posts, whitepapers, and videos can position us as thought leaders and drive organic traffic," he said. "Content marketing also supports our SEO efforts and provides material for social media and email campaigns."

Emma proposed leveraging paid advertising to amplify their reach. "Paid campaigns on platforms like Google Ads, LinkedIn Ads, and Facebook Ads can help us target specific audience segments and achieve quick results," she noted. "We can use retargeting to stay top-of-mind for potential customers."

As they evaluated each channel, a clear picture began to emerge of a multi-channel strategy that balanced organic and paid efforts, leveraging both digital and traditional channels.

David suggested setting up a system for tracking channel performance. "We need to monitor key metrics for each channel to understand what's working and where we need to make adjustments," he said. "This will help us allocate our resources more effectively and optimize our strategy over time."

Emma proposed creating a content calendar to coordinate their efforts. "A content calendar ensures that our messaging is consistent across all channels and helps us plan our campaigns strategically," she remarked. "It also allows us to track our progress and stay on schedule."

With their channel strategy defined, the team felt a renewed sense of confidence and direction. They understood that choosing the right channels was critical for maximizing the impact of their marketing efforts and achieving their goals.

As they left the conference room, Emma, David, Lisa, and the rest of the team felt a surge of excitement. They knew that by strategically selecting and leveraging the right channels, they could effectively reach their target audience and drive meaningful engagement. Together, they would embark on a journey where every channel echoed their brand narrative, guiding their audience towards shared success and fostering a lasting connection with InnovateTech.

Content Marketing Strategies

The InnovateTech conference room was once again filled with a sense of purpose as the leadership team gathered to discuss the heart of their marketing efforts: content marketing strategies. Emma, David, Lisa, and their colleagues were ready to craft compelling content that would not only capture the attention of their audience but also drive engagement and loyalty.

Lisa, the CEO, stood at the front with a determined expression. "We've set our goals and chosen our channels. Now, it's time to focus on content marketing strategies," she began. "Content is the cornerstone of our engagement efforts. It's how we tell our story and connect with our audience on a deeper level."

David, ever the analytical thinker, nodded. "Effective content marketing requires a strategic approach," he remarked. "We need to create content that is valuable, relevant, and consistent. It should not only attract our target audience but also encourage them to take action."

Emma, the strategist, interjected with enthusiasm. "Let's start by defining the types of content that resonate most with our audience," she suggested. "We need to consider different formats such as blog posts, videos, infographics, e-books, and social media updates."

Lisa clicked her remote, and the projector displayed a content matrix. "We need to map out our content strategy," she said. "Starting with our key messages, we'll outline how we can convey them through different content formats across various channels."

As they embarked on the task, the team discussed the importance of aligning their content with their audience's needs and preferences.

David highlighted the value of educational content. "Our audience looks to us for expertise," he noted. "Creating how-to guides, industry reports, and whitepapers can position us as thought leaders and provide valuable insights to our audience."

Emma echoed his sentiment, "Visual content like videos and infographics can engage our audience more effectively, especially on social media platforms. We can create behind-the-scenes videos, product demonstrations, and customer testimonials to showcase our brand."

Lisa emphasized the need for storytelling in their content. "Stories resonate with people on an emotional level," she remarked. "We should share stories about our brand's journey, our team, and our customers. Highlighting real-life experiences can create a stronger connection with our audience."

David suggested leveraging user-generated content to amplify their efforts. "Encouraging our customers to share their stories and experiences with our products can provide authentic and relatable content," he said. "User-generated content also builds community and trust."

Emma proposed creating a content calendar to plan and organize their efforts. "A content calendar helps us maintain consistency and ensure that we're delivering a steady stream of content across all channels," she remarked. "It also allows us to coordinate our campaigns and track our progress."

With their content strategy taking shape, the team turned their attention to distribution and promotion.

Lisa highlighted the importance of SEO in content marketing. "Optimizing our content for search engines can drive organic traffic to our website," she noted. "We need to conduct keyword research and ensure that our content aligns with the search intent of our audience."

David suggested using social media and email marketing to distribute their content. "Promoting our content through social media channels and email campaigns can extend its reach and drive engagement," he said. "We can also collaborate with influencers to amplify our message."

Emma emphasized the need for continuous improvement. "We should regularly review our content performance and gather feedback from our audience," she remarked. "This will help us refine our strategy and ensure that we're delivering content that resonates."

As they meticulously outlined their content marketing strategy, a sense of excitement and anticipation filled the room. They were embarking on a journey to create compelling and valuable content that would engage their audience and drive their marketing goals.

With their strategy in place, Emma, David, Lisa, and the rest of the team left the conference room with a renewed sense of purpose. They understood that by crafting and distributing high-quality content, they could forge meaningful connections with their audience and propel InnovateTech towards success. Together, they would embark on a journey where every piece of content echoed their brand narrative, guiding their audience towards shared prosperity and building lasting relationships.

Social Media Marketing

The InnovateTech conference room was filled with a palpable sense of excitement as the leadership team gathered to focus on the next crucial aspect of their marketing strategy: social media marketing. Emma, David, Lisa, and their colleagues were ready to harness the power of social media to amplify their brand narrative and engage their audience in dynamic, meaningful ways.

Lisa, the CEO, stood at the front with a confident demeanor.

"Social media marketing is our next frontier," she began. "It's where we can truly connect with our audience, build our community, and amplify our brand story."

David, ever the data-driven thinker, nodded thoughtfully. "Social media offers a unique opportunity to reach and engage our audience in real-time," he remarked. "But we need a strategic approach to ensure our efforts are impactful and aligned with our goals."

Emma, the strategist, interjected with enthusiasm. "Let's start by identifying the platforms that align best with our target audience," she suggested. "We need to consider where our audience spends their time and how they prefer to interact with content."

Lisa clicked her remote, and the projector displayed a list of potential social media platforms. "We'll evaluate each platform based on its user demographics, engagement features, and relevance to our brand," she said.

As they embarked on the task, the team discussed the strengths and opportunities presented by different social media channels.

David highlighted the power of LinkedIn for B2B engagement. "LinkedIn is ideal for reaching professionals and decision-makers," he noted. "We can share industry insights, company updates, and thought leadership content to build credibility and connect with potential clients."

Emma echoed his sentiment, "Instagram and Facebook offer great opportunities for visual storytelling and community building. We can use these platforms to share behind-the-scenes content, customer stories, and engage with our audience through comments and direct messages."

Lisa emphasized the importance of Twitter for real-time engagement. "Twitter allows us to participate in conversations, share timely updates, and engage with industry influencers," she remarked. "It's a powerful platform for building our brand voice and staying relevant."

David suggested leveraging YouTube for video content. "Videos are highly engaging and can convey our brand story effectively," he said. "We can create product demonstrations, tutorials, and customer testimonials to showcase our expertise and value."

Emma proposed a content plan for each platform. "We need to tailor our content to fit the strengths of each platform," she remarked. "For LinkedIn, we focus on professional insights; for Instagram, visual storytelling; for Twitter, timely updates; and for YouTube, in-depth videos."

As they outlined their social media strategy, the team turned their attention to engagement and community building.

Lisa highlighted the importance of authentic interaction. "Engagement is not just about posting content; it's about building relationships," she noted. "We need to respond to comments, participate in discussions, and show our audience that we value their input."

David suggested using analytics to track their social media performance. "We need to monitor key metrics like engagement rate, follower growth, and conversion rate to understand what works and where we can improve," he said. "Regular analysis will help us refine our strategy."

Emma emphasized the need for a consistent posting schedule. "Consistency is key to maintaining our audience's interest," she remarked. "We should create a social media calendar to plan our posts and ensure we're delivering a steady stream of content."

With their social media strategy defined, the team felt a surge of confidence and enthusiasm. They understood that by leveraging social media effectively, they could amplify their brand narrative, engage their audience, and drive meaningful interactions.

As they left the conference room, Emma, David, Lisa, and the rest of the team felt a renewed sense of purpose. They knew that by harnessing the power of social media, they could create a vibrant community and foster deeper connections with their audience. Together, they would embark on a journey where every social media post echoed their brand narrative, guiding their audience towards shared success and building lasting relationships with InnovateTech.

Email Marketing Campaigns

The InnovateTech conference room was once again alive with anticipation as the leadership team gathered to discuss the next crucial aspect of their marketing strategy: email marketing campaigns. Emma, David, Lisa, and their colleagues were eager to craft personalized email campaigns that would foster deeper connections with their audience and drive engagement.

Lisa, the CEO, began with a sense of urgency. "Email marketing is one of the most direct ways to reach our audience," she started. "It's about creating personalized and relevant communications that resonate with our subscribers and drive action."

David, the analytical thinker, nodded. "Emails allow us to deliver targeted messages directly to our audience's inbox," he remarked. "We need to focus on creating compelling content and segmenting our audience to ensure relevance."

Emma, the strategist, chimed in with enthusiasm. "Let's start by defining our goals for email marketing," she suggested. "Are we focusing on lead nurturing, customer retention, or driving sales? We need to tailor our campaigns accordingly."

Lisa clicked her remote, displaying a framework for email marketing strategy on the projector. "We'll begin by segmenting our audience based on their behavior, interests, and demographics," she said. "This allows us to send highly targeted and relevant emails."

The team discussed the various types of email campaigns they could implement.

David highlighted the importance of welcome emails. "Welcome emails are our first opportunity to make a great impression," he noted. "We should introduce our brand, set expectations, and provide value right from the start."

Emma suggested implementing a series of nurturing emails. "Nurturing emails can guide our leads through the buyer's journey," she said. "We can provide educational content, case studies, and product information to help them make informed decisions."

Lisa emphasized the value of promotional emails. "Promotional emails can drive sales and engagement," she remarked. "We can offer exclusive discounts, announce new products, and create a sense of urgency with limited-time offers."

David proposed using re-engagement emails to retain subscribers. "Re-engagement emails can win back inactive subscribers," he said. "We can remind them of the value we provide and offer incentives to bring them back."

Emma recommended personalized emails for customer retention. "Personalized emails can enhance customer loyalty," she remarked. "We can send birthday greetings, product recommendations based on past purchases, and thank-you notes."

As they outlined their email marketing strategy, the team turned their attention to content creation and optimization.

Lisa highlighted the importance of compelling subject lines. "The subject line is the first thing our audience sees," she noted. "It needs to be intriguing and relevant to encourage opens."

David suggested optimizing email content for mobile devices. "Many people check their emails on mobile devices," he said. "We need to ensure our emails are mobile-friendly and easy to read."

Emma emphasized the need for clear calls-to-action. "Each email should have a clear and compelling call-to-action," she remarked. "Whether it's visiting our website, downloading a resource, or making a purchase, we need to guide our audience towards the next step."

With their email marketing strategy defined, the team felt a renewed sense of confidence. They understood that by crafting personalized and relevant email campaigns, they could foster deeper connections with their audience and drive meaningful engagement.

Influencer and Partnership Marketing

As the meeting transitioned to the final subpoint of Chapter 5, the InnovateTech conference room remained charged with enthusiasm. The leadership team was now ready to explore influencer and partnership marketing, a strategy aimed at leveraging external voices to amplify their brand reach.

Lisa, the CEO, took the lead. "Influencer and partnership

marketing can significantly extend our reach and credibility," she began. "By collaborating with influencers and partners who align with our brand values, we can tap into their established audiences and build trust."

David, the data-driven strategist, nodded. "Influencers can provide authentic endorsements and create engaging content that resonates with their followers," he remarked. "Partnerships with complementary brands can open new avenues for growth and visibility."

Emma, ever the visionary, interjected with excitement. "Let's start by identifying potential influencers and partners who align with our brand and audience," she suggested. "We need to consider their reach, engagement, and relevance to our target market."

Lisa clicked her remote, displaying a list of potential influencers and partners. "We'll evaluate each candidate based on their alignment with our brand values, audience demographics, and engagement rates," she said.

The team discussed their criteria for selecting influencers and partners.

David highlighted the importance of authenticity. "We need influencers who genuinely resonate with their followers and have built trust over time," he noted. "Authenticity is key to ensuring their endorsements are effective."

Emma suggested looking for influencers who create high-quality content. "Quality content enhances our brand image and engagement," she said. "We should look for influencers who consistently produce visually appealing and informative content."

Lisa emphasized the value of shared goals and values with partners. "Partnerships should be mutually beneficial," she remarked. "We need to find partners whose values and goals align with ours, creating a synergy that benefits both parties."

David proposed setting clear objectives for each collaboration. "Whether it's increasing brand awareness, driving traffic, or boosting sales, we need to define our goals upfront," he said. "Clear objectives will guide our collaborations and help measure success."

Emma recommended creating unique and engaging campaigns with influencers. "Influencers can bring creativity and authenticity to our campaigns," she remarked. "We can co-create content that showcases our products in real-life scenarios, making it more relatable and impactful."

As they outlined their influencer and partnership marketing strategy, the team turned their attention to execution and measurement.

Lisa highlighted the importance of maintaining strong relationships with influencers and partners. "Building long-term relationships can lead to ongoing collaborations and deeper connections with their audiences," she noted. "We should communicate regularly and support each other's goals."

David suggested using performance metrics to evaluate the success of each collaboration. "We need to track key metrics such as engagement rates, website traffic, and conversion rates to understand the impact of our collaborations," he said. "Regular analysis will help us refine our strategy."

Emma emphasized the need for transparency and authenticity in all collaborations. "Transparency builds trust with our audience," she remarked. "We should clearly disclose our partnerships and ensure that all collaborations align with our brand values and messaging."

With their influencer and partnership marketing strategy

defined, the team felt a surge of excitement and anticipation. They understood that by leveraging the power of influencers and strategic partnerships, they could amplify their brand reach and build trust with new audiences.

As they left the conference room, Emma, David, Lisa, and the rest of the team felt a renewed sense of purpose. They knew that by collaborating with the right influencers and partners, they could create impactful campaigns that resonated with their audience and drove growth. Together, they would embark on a journey where every collaboration echoed their brand narrative, guiding their audience towards shared success and building lasting relationships with InnovateTech.

6

Chapter 6: Creating a Powerful Sales Strategy

Building a Robust Sales Funnel

The InnovateTech conference room was filled with a determined energy as the leadership team gathered to tackle the next phase of their strategic planning: creating a powerful sales strategy. Emma, David, Lisa, and their colleagues knew that building a robust sales funnel was crucial for converting prospects into loyal customers.

Lisa, the CEO, stood at the front with an air of confidence. "We've laid a strong foundation with our marketing strategies," she began. "Now, it's time to focus on our sales strategy, starting with building a robust sales funnel. This funnel will guide our prospects through the buying journey, from initial awareness to final purchase."

David, the analytical thinker, nodded thoughtfully. "A well-structured sales funnel is essential for nurturing leads and converting them into customers," he remarked. "We need to understand each stage of the funnel and develop strategies to move prospects through each phase."

Emma, the strategist, interjected with enthusiasm. "Let's start by defining the stages of our sales funnel," she suggested. "We need to map out the journey our prospects take, from awareness to consideration, decision, and finally, action."

Lisa clicked her remote, and the projector displayed a diagram of a sales funnel. "We'll focus on four key stages: Awareness, Interest, Decision, and Action," she said. "Each stage requires specific tactics to engage and nurture our prospects."

The team delved into the details of each stage, discussing strategies and tactics to effectively guide their prospects through the funnel.

Awareness Stage

David highlighted the importance of creating awareness. "In the awareness stage, our goal is to attract and capture the attention of potential customers," he noted. "We can use content marketing, social media, and SEO to increase our visibility and drive traffic to our website."

Emma suggested using educational content to build awareness. "We can create blog posts, videos, and infographics that address common pain points and provide valuable insights," she said. "This positions us as a trusted resource and draws prospects into our funnel."

Interest Stage

Lisa emphasized the need to nurture interest. "Once we've captured their attention, we need to keep our prospects engaged and interested in our offerings," she remarked. "We can use email marketing, webinars, and personalized content to nurture their interest."

David proposed using lead magnets to capture contact information. "Offering valuable resources such as e-books, whitepapers, and free trials in exchange for contact information can help us build our email list," he said. "This allows us to continue nurturing our prospects with targeted content."

Decision Stage

Emma focused on guiding prospects towards a decision. "In the decision stage, our goal is to provide the information and reassurance they need to choose our products or services," she noted. "We can use case studies, product demos, and customer testimonials to build trust and credibility."

Lisa suggested offering personalized consultations. "Personalized consultations can address specific needs and concerns, helping prospects see the value of our solutions," she said. "This personal touch can make a significant difference in their decision-making process."

Action Stage

David highlighted the importance of facilitating action. "In the action stage, we need to make it as easy as possible for prospects to make a purchase," he remarked. "We can use clear calls-to-action, seamless checkout processes, and special offers to encourage conversions."

Emma proposed implementing retargeting campaigns. "Retargeting campaigns can remind prospects of the value we offer and nudge them towards completing their purchase," she said. "We can use targeted ads and follow-up emails to stay top-of-mind."

As they outlined their sales funnel strategy, the team felt a surge of confidence and excitement. They understood that by building a robust sales funnel, they could effectively guide their prospects through the buying journey and convert them into loyal customers.

Lisa emphasized the importance of continuous optimization. "We need to regularly review and optimize our sales funnel," she remarked. "By analyzing data and gathering feedback, we can identify areas for improvement and ensure our funnel remains effective."

David suggested using analytics to track key metrics. "We need to monitor metrics such as conversion rates, lead quality, and sales cycle length to understand the performance of our funnel," he said. "Regular analysis will help us refine our strategies and achieve better results."

Emma recommended aligning sales and marketing efforts. "Collaboration between our sales and marketing teams is crucial for a seamless funnel," she noted. "We need to ensure that our messaging is consistent and that our teams are working towards shared goals."

With their sales funnel strategy defined, the team felt a renewed sense of purpose. They knew that by building a robust sales funnel, they could effectively nurture their prospects and drive meaningful engagement and conversions.

As they left the conference room, Emma, David, Lisa, and the rest of the team felt a sense of determination and excitement. They understood that by creating a powerful sales strategy, they could propel InnovateTech towards greater success. Together, they would embark on a journey where every stage of the sales funnel echoed their brand narrative, guiding their prospects towards shared prosperity and building lasting relationships with InnovateTech.

Lead Generation Techniques

The InnovateTech conference room was buzzing with energy as the leadership team gathered once again, this time to dive into the critical topic of lead generation techniques. Emma, David, Lisa, and their colleagues were ready to explore innovative ways to attract and capture high-quality leads that would fuel their sales funnel.

Lisa, the CEO, stood at the front with a determined expression. "Lead generation is the lifeblood of our sales strategy," she began. "We need a diverse set of techniques to attract potential customers and bring them into our funnel. Let's brainstorm effective ways to generate leads."

David, the analytical thinker, nodded thoughtfully. "Effective lead generation requires a multi-channel approach," he remarked. "We need to reach our audience where they are and offer value that compels them to take action."

Emma, the strategist, interjected with enthusiasm. "Let's start by exploring digital marketing techniques," she suggested. "Online channels offer a wealth of opportunities for reaching our target audience and capturing leads."

Lisa clicked her remote, and the projector displayed a list of lead generation techniques. "We'll focus on a combination of inbound and outbound strategies," she said. "Each technique should align with our overall marketing goals and target audience."

Content Marketing

Emma highlighted the importance of content marketing for lead generation. "High-quality content can attract and engage our target audience," she noted. "We can create blog posts, e-books, whitepapers, and videos that address their pain points and provide valuable insights."

David suggested using gated content to capture leads. "Offering valuable resources in exchange for contact information is an effective way to generate leads," he said. "We can use forms and landing pages to capture details from interested prospects."

Social Media Marketing

Lisa emphasized the role of social media in lead generation. "Social media platforms offer a direct way to reach and engage our audience," she remarked. "We can use targeted ads, sponsored posts, and organic content to drive traffic to our website and capture leads."

Emma proposed using social media contests and giveaways. "Contests and giveaways can create excitement and encourage participation," she said. "We can require participants to provide their contact information to enter, generating a list of potential leads."

SEO and SEM

David focused on search engine optimization (SEO) and search engine marketing (SEM). "Optimizing our website for search engines can drive organic traffic and capture leads," he noted. "We can use keyword research, on-page SEO, and high-quality content to improve our rankings."

Lisa suggested using pay-per-click (PPC) advertising for lead generation. "PPC ads can drive targeted traffic to our landing pages," she said. "We can create ads that address specific search queries and direct users to forms or contact pages."

Email Marketing

Emma highlighted the value of email marketing for lead generation. "Email campaigns can nurture prospects and drive them towards taking action," she remarked. "We can use lead magnets, personalized content, and automated workflows to capture and nurture leads."

David proposed implementing a referral program. "Encouraging our existing customers to refer new leads can be highly effective," he said. "We can offer incentives for referrals, creating a win-win situation for our customers and our business."

Webinars and Events

Lisa emphasized the importance of hosting webinars and events. "Webinars and events provide a platform for us to share our expertise and engage with our audience," she noted. "We can require registration for these events, capturing contact information from interested participants."

Emma suggested partnering with industry influencers for co-hosted webinars. "Collaborating with influencers can extend our reach and attract a larger audience," she said. "Co-hosted webinars can provide valuable insights and generate high-quality leads."

Lead Nurturing

David focused on the importance of lead nurturing. "Capturing leads is only the first step," he noted. "We need to nurture those leads through targeted email campaigns, personalized content, and ongoing engagement to convert them into customers."

Lisa emphasized the need for a lead scoring system. "Lead scoring can help us prioritize our efforts," she said. "By assigning scores based on engagement and behavior, we can identify high-potential leads and focus our resources on nurturing them."

As they outlined their lead generation strategy, the team felt a renewed sense of excitement and confidence. They understood that by implementing a diverse set of lead generation techniques, they could attract and capture high-quality leads to fuel their sales funnel.

Emma highlighted the importance of continuous improvement. "We need to regularly review and optimize our lead generation efforts," she remarked. "By analyzing data and gathering feedback, we can identify areas for improvement and ensure our techniques remain effective."

David suggested using analytics to track the performance

of each technique. "We need to monitor key metrics such as conversion rates, cost per lead, and lead quality," he said. "Regular analysis will help us refine our strategies and achieve better results."

With their lead generation strategy defined, the team felt a renewed sense of purpose. They knew that by implementing a diverse set of techniques, they could attract and capture high-quality leads that would drive growth for InnovateTech.

As they left the conference room, Emma, David, Lisa, and the rest of the team felt a sense of determination and excitement. They understood that by creating a powerful sales strategy with robust lead generation techniques, they could propel InnovateTech towards greater success. Together, they would embark on a journey where every lead generation effort echoed their brand narrative, guiding their prospects towards shared prosperity and building lasting relationships with InnovateTech.

Prospecting and Outreach Methods

The InnovateTech conference room was abuzz with activity as the leadership team reconvened to tackle the next critical component of their sales strategy: prospecting and outreach methods. Emma, David, Lisa, and their colleagues were eager to refine their approach to identify and engage potential customers effectively.

Lisa, the CEO, began the session with a sense of urgency. "Prospecting and outreach are vital for maintaining a steady flow of qualified leads into our sales funnel," she said. "We need to be strategic and proactive in our efforts to connect with potential customers."

David, the analytical thinker, nodded. "Effective prospecting and outreach require a mix of techniques and a deep understanding of our target audience," he remarked. "We need to personalize our approach and make meaningful connections."

Emma, the strategist, interjected with enthusiasm. "Let's start by identifying key prospecting methods," she suggested. "We need to find the right balance between traditional and digital techniques to reach our audience effectively."

Lisa clicked her remote, and the projector displayed a list of prospecting and outreach methods. "We'll focus on six main techniques: cold calling, email outreach, social selling, networking, referrals, and direct mail," she said. "Each method should be tailored to our target audience and goals."

Cold Calling

Emma highlighted the role of cold calling in prospecting. "Cold calling can be an effective way to reach potential customers directly," she noted. "We need to prepare a compelling script, anticipate objections, and focus on building rapport."

David suggested using a research-driven approach. "Before making a call, we should research the prospect's company and industry," he said. "Understanding their needs and pain points will help us tailor our pitch and demonstrate value."

Lisa emphasized the importance of persistence. "Cold calling often requires multiple attempts to reach a decision-maker," she remarked. "We need to be persistent but respectful, following up regularly without being intrusive."

Email Outreach

Emma focused on email outreach as a key method. "Email outreach allows us to send personalized messages to a large number of prospects," she said. "We need to craft engaging subject lines and compelling content that resonates with our audience."

David proposed using automation tools to streamline the process. "Email automation tools can help us manage our outreach campaigns and track responses," he noted. "We can create sequences that follow up with prospects automatically, ensuring consistent communication."

Lisa suggested using a mix of content in email outreach. "We can share valuable resources such as case studies, industry insights, and product information," she said. "Providing value in our emails will help build trust and keep prospects engaged."

Social Selling

Emma highlighted the importance of social selling. "Social media platforms offer a unique opportunity to connect with prospects and build relationships," she remarked. "We need to engage with our audience by sharing relevant content, participating in discussions, and reaching out directly."

David suggested using LinkedIn for B2B prospecting. "LinkedIn is a powerful tool for B2B outreach," he said. "We can use advanced search filters to find potential customers, send personalized connection requests, and engage with their content."

Lisa emphasized the need for authenticity. "Authenticity is key in social selling," she remarked. "We should focus on building genuine relationships rather than just making a sale. This approach will create lasting connections and trust."

Networking

Emma focused on the value of networking. "Attending industry events, conferences, and meetups can help us connect with potential customers and industry influencers," she noted. "We need to be proactive in seeking out opportunities to network."

David proposed creating a structured approach to networking. "We should set clear goals for each event and prepare an elevator pitch," he said. "Following up with contacts after the event is crucial for maintaining the relationship."

Lisa suggested leveraging online networking opportunities. "In addition to in-person events, we can participate in webinars, online forums, and virtual conferences," she said. "These platforms offer valuable networking opportunities and can expand our reach."

Referrals

Emma highlighted the importance of referrals. "Referrals from satisfied customers and partners can be highly effective," she remarked. "We need to create a referral program that incentivizes our customers to recommend us to their network."

David suggested tracking and rewarding successful referrals. "We can offer rewards such as discounts, gift cards, or exclusive access to new products," he said. "Tracking referral success will help us understand the impact and refine our program."

Lisa emphasized the need for a personalized approach. "When reaching out to referred prospects, we should mention the referrer and highlight the value we can provide," she remarked. "This personalized touch can make a significant difference in our outreach."

Direct Mail

Emma focused on the potential of direct mail. "Direct mail can stand out in a digital world," she noted. "We can send personalized letters, brochures, and promotional items to capture the attention of our prospects."

David proposed using a targeted approach. "We should focus on high-potential prospects and tailor our direct mail to their specific needs and interests," he said. "Follow-up calls or emails can reinforce our message and drive engagement."

Lisa suggested incorporating creative elements. "Creative direct mail pieces can leave a lasting impression," she remarked. "We can use unique packaging, personalized messages, and interactive elements to engage our prospects."

As they outlined their prospecting and outreach strategy, the team felt a renewed sense of confidence and excitement. They understood that by employing a diverse set of techniques, they could effectively connect with potential customers and fuel their sales funnel.

Emma emphasized the importance of continuous optimization. "We need to regularly review and refine our prospecting and outreach efforts," she remarked. "By analyzing data and gathering feedback, we can identify areas for improvement and ensure our techniques remain effective."

David suggested using analytics to track key metrics. "We need to monitor metrics such as response rates, conversion rates, and lead quality," he said. "Regular analysis will help us refine our strategies and achieve better results."

With their prospecting and outreach strategy defined, the team felt a renewed sense of purpose. They knew that by employing a diverse set of techniques, they could effectively connect with potential customers and drive growth for InnovateTech.

As they left the conference room, Emma, David, Lisa, and the rest of the team felt a sense of determination and excitement. They understood that by creating a powerful sales strategy with effective prospecting and outreach methods, they could propel InnovateTech towards greater success. Together, they would embark on a journey where every prospecting effort echoed their brand narrative, guiding their prospects towards shared prosperity and building lasting relationships with InnovateTech.

Sales Pitch and Presentation Skills

The InnovateTech conference room was alive with anticipation as the leadership team gathered to refine their sales pitch and presentation skills. Emma, David, Lisa, and their colleagues knew that mastering these skills was crucial for converting leads into loyal customers.

Lisa, the CEO, started the session with a determined tone. "Delivering a compelling sales pitch and presentation can make or break a deal," she began. "We need to captivate our audience, address their needs, and convincingly present the value of our solutions."

David, the analytical thinker, nodded thoughtfully. "Our pitch needs to be clear, concise, and tailored to our audience," he remarked. "We should focus on understanding our prospects' pain points and demonstrating how our solutions address them."

Emma, the strategist, interjected with enthusiasm. "Let's start by crafting our core pitch," she suggested. "We need a narrative that highlights our unique value proposition and resonates with our target audience."

Lisa clicked her remote, and the projector displayed a list of key elements for a successful sales pitch and presentation. "We'll focus on six main aspects: understanding the audience, crafting a compelling narrative, using visual aids effectively, practicing delivery, handling objections, and closing with confidence," she said. "Each element is crucial for a successful presentation."

Understanding the Audience

Emma highlighted the importance of audience research. "Before we can deliver a compelling pitch, we need to understand who we're speaking to," she noted. "Researching the prospect's company, industry, and specific challenges will help us tailor our message."

David suggested creating customized pitches for different audience segments. "We can develop tailored presentations for different industries, company sizes, and decision-maker roles," he said. "Personalization will make our pitch more relevant and impactful."

Lisa emphasized the need to listen actively. "During the presentation, we should encourage dialogue and listen to our prospects' concerns," she remarked. "Active listening will help us address their needs more effectively."

Crafting a Compelling Narrative

Emma focused on the power of storytelling. "A compelling narrative can captivate our audience and make our pitch memorable," she said. "We need to create a story that highlights the benefits of our solutions and connects with our prospects emotionally."

David proposed using a problem-solution framework. "We can start by outlining the prospect's challenges and then present our solutions as the answer," he noted. "This approach helps to clearly demonstrate the value we offer."

Lisa suggested incorporating customer success stories. "Sharing real-life examples of how our solutions have helped other customers can build credibility," she remarked. "Testimonials and case studies can make our pitch more persuasive."

Using Visual Aids Effectively

Emma highlighted the importance of visual aids. "Visual aids can enhance our presentation and make complex information more accessible," she noted. "We need to use slides, charts, and graphics to support our narrative and keep our audience engaged."

David suggested keeping slides simple and focused. "Our slides should complement our verbal message, not overwhelm it," he said. "We should use minimal text, clear visuals, and highlight key points."

Lisa emphasized the need for consistency in design. "Consistent branding and design throughout our presentation will make it more professional," she remarked. "We should use our company's colors, fonts, and logos to reinforce our brand identity."

Practicing Delivery

Emma focused on the importance of practice. "Delivering a confident and polished presentation requires practice," she said. "We need to rehearse our pitch multiple times, both individually and as a team."

David proposed using role-playing exercises. "Role-playing can help us anticipate questions and objections," he noted. "We can simulate different scenarios and practice our responses to build confidence."

Lisa suggested recording practice sessions for review. "Recording our practice sessions allows us to analyze our delivery and make improvements," she remarked. "We can identify areas for improvement and refine our approach."

Handling Objections

Emma highlighted the need to handle objections gracefully. "Objections are a natural part of the sales process," she noted. "We need to listen to our prospects' concerns, empathize with them, and provide clear, thoughtful responses."

David suggested preparing for common objections. "We can create a list of common objections and develop well-thought-out responses," he said. "This preparation will help us address concerns confidently and effectively."

Lisa emphasized the importance of staying positive. "We should remain positive and solution-focused when handling objections," she remarked. "Demonstrating empathy and understanding can turn objections into opportunities for deeper engagement."

Closing with Confidence

Emma focused on the importance of a strong close. "A powerful closing can leave a lasting impression and drive action," she said. "We need to summarize our key points, reinforce the value of our solutions, and provide a clear call to action."

David proposed using closing techniques such as the assumptive close. "The assumptive close involves assuming the prospect is ready to move forward," he noted. "Phrases like 'When we get started…' can create a sense of inevitability and momentum."

Lisa suggested leaving room for follow-up. "We should provide opportunities for follow-up discussions," she remarked. "Scheduling a follow-up meeting or call demonstrates our commitment to their success and keeps the conversation going."

As they outlined their sales pitch and presentation strategy, the team felt a renewed sense of confidence and excitement. They understood that by mastering these skills, they could effectively engage with potential customers and drive meaningful conversions.

Emma emphasized the importance of continuous improvement. "We need to regularly review and refine our sales pitch and presentation skills," she remarked. "By gathering feedback and analyzing performance, we can identify areas for improvement and ensure our techniques remain effective."

David suggested using analytics to track key metrics. "We need to monitor metrics such as presentation success rates, conversion rates, and customer feedback," he said. "Regular analysis will help us refine our strategies and achieve better results."

With their sales pitch and presentation strategy defined, the team felt a renewed sense of purpose. They knew that by mastering these skills, they could effectively engage with potential customers and drive growth for InnovateTech.

As they left the conference room, Emma, David, Lisa, and the rest of the team felt a sense of determination and excitement. They understood that by creating a powerful sales strategy with compelling sales pitches and presentations, they could propel InnovateTech towards greater success. Together, they would embark on a journey where every pitch echoed their brand narrative, guiding their prospects towards shared prosperity and building lasting relationships with InnovateTech.

Negotiation and Closing Techniques

The atmosphere in the InnovateTech conference room was charged with anticipation as the leadership team gathered to delve into the intricacies of negotiation and closing techniques. Emma, David, Lisa, and their colleagues knew that mastering these skills was essential for sealing deals and driving business growth.

Lisa, the CEO, opened the session with a determined tone. "Negotiation and closing are critical stages of the sales process," she began. "We need to approach these interactions with confidence, tact, and a focus on mutual value creation."

David, the analytical thinker, nodded in agreement. "Effective negotiation requires a deep understanding of our prospects' needs and priorities," he remarked. "We need to be prepared to adapt our approach and find win-win solutions."

Emma, the strategist, interjected with enthusiasm. "Let's start by exploring negotiation techniques," she suggested. "We need to be proactive, assertive, and strategic in our negotiations to achieve favorable outcomes."

Lisa clicked her remote, and the projector displayed a list of key elements for successful negotiation and closing techniques. "We'll focus on six main aspects: preparation, active listening, building rapport, managing objections, closing strategies, and post-close follow-up," she said. "Each element is crucial for navigating the negotiation process effectively."

Preparation

Emma highlighted the importance of preparation in negotiation. "Before entering into negotiations, we need to research the prospect's needs, preferences, and potential objections," she noted. "Having a clear understanding of their goals and constraints will allow us to tailor our approach and anticipate potential challenges."

David suggested creating a negotiation plan. "We should outline our objectives, desired outcomes, and potential concessions," he said. "A well-defined plan will keep us focused and confident during the negotiation process."

Lisa emphasized the need to set clear boundaries. "We should establish our non-negotiables and priorities before entering into negotiations," she remarked. "Having a clear understanding of our limits will prevent us from making concessions that compromise our interests."

Active Listening

Emma focused on the importance of active listening in negotiation. "Effective negotiation requires us to listen carefully to our prospect's concerns, interests, and priorities," she said. "We should ask probing questions and demonstrate empathy to gain a deeper understanding of their perspective."

David suggested using reflective listening techniques. "We can paraphrase and summarize our prospect's statements to show that we understand their point of view," he noted. "This builds rapport and trust, laying the foundation for productive negotiations."

Lisa emphasized the need to validate the prospect's feelings. "Acknowledging and validating our prospect's concerns can help defuse tension and build rapport," she remarked. "We should show empathy and understanding, even if we don't agree with their perspective."

Building Rapport

Emma highlighted the importance of building rapport in negotiation. "Establishing a positive rapport with our prospect creates a foundation of trust and mutual respect," she noted. "We should find common ground, share personal anecdotes, and be genuine in our interactions."

David suggested using humor strategically. "Humor can lighten the mood and break down barriers," he said. "We should use humor sparingly and ensure that it aligns with our prospect's personality and cultural context."

Lisa emphasized the value of body language. "Our body language communicates as much as our words," she remarked. "We should maintain open and confident posture, make eye contact, and nod in agreement to signal active listening."

Managing Objections

Emma focused on the importance of addressing objections effectively. "Objections are a natural part of the negotiation process," she noted. "We should listen attentively to our prospect's concerns, acknowledge them, and respond with confidence and empathy."

David suggested reframing objections as opportunities. "We can use objections as a chance to provide additional information and clarify misunderstandings," he said. "By reframing objections as opportunities for discussion, we can keep the negotiation moving forward."

Lisa emphasized the need for flexibility. "We should be prepared to adapt our approach and find creative solutions to overcome objections," she remarked. "Flexibility and willingness to compromise can lead to mutually beneficial outcomes."

Closing Strategies

Emma highlighted the importance of closing effectively. "The closing stage is where we seal the deal and secure commitment from our prospect," she said. "We should summarize the key points, address any remaining concerns, and propose a clear next step."

David suggested using assumptive language. "Phrases like 'When we move forward…' or 'As we finalize the details…' can create a sense of inevitability and encourage the prospect to commit," he noted. "Assumptive language signals confidence and reinforces the prospect's decision."

Lisa emphasized the value of urgency. "Creating a sense of urgency can motivate the prospect to take action," she remarked. "We should highlight time-sensitive benefits or limited-time offers to encourage prompt decision-making."

Post-Close Follow-Up

Emma focused on the importance of post-close follow-up. "After securing commitment, we need to follow up promptly to ensure a smooth transition and reinforce the prospect's decision," she said. "We should express appreciation, provide additional information if needed, and confirm next steps."

David suggested using a personalized approach to follow-up. "We should tailor our follow-up communications to the prospect's preferences and communication style," he noted. "Personalized emails or handwritten notes can leave a positive impression and strengthen the relationship."

Lisa emphasized the need for ongoing engagement. "Our relationship with the prospect doesn't end after the close," she remarked. "We should continue to provide value, support, and proactive communication to build trust and loyalty."

As they outlined their negotiation and closing techniques, the team felt a renewed sense of confidence and excitement. They understood that by mastering these skills, they could navigate the negotiation process effectively and drive meaningful outcomes for InnovateTech.

Emma emphasized the importance of continuous improvement. "We need to regularly review and refine our negotiation and closing techniques," she remarked. "By gathering feedback and analyzing performance, we can identify areas for improvement and ensure our approaches remain effective."

David suggested using analytics to track key metrics. "We need to monitor metrics such as deal close rates, deal size, and customer satisfaction scores," he said. "Regular analysis will help us refine our strategies and achieve better results."

With their negotiation and closing techniques defined, the team felt a renewed sense of purpose. They knew that by mastering these skills, they could effectively navigate the negotiation process and drive growth for InnovateTech.

As they left the conference room, Emma, David, Lisa, and the rest of the team felt a sense of determination and excitement. They understood that by creating a powerful sales strategy with effective negotiation and closing techniques, they could propel InnovateTech towards greater success. Together, they would embark on a journey where every negotiation echoed their brand narrative, guiding their prospects towards shared prosperity and building lasting relationships with InnovateTech.

Post-Sale Follow-Up

In the InnovateTech conference room, the atmosphere hummed with anticipation as the leadership team gathered to discuss the final piece of their sales strategy puzzle: post-sale follow-up. Emma, David, Lisa, and their colleagues knew that the journey didn't end with closing a deal; it continued with nurturing relationships and ensuring customer satisfaction.

Lisa, the CEO, set the tone with a sense of determination. "Post-sale follow-up is crucial for fostering long-term relationships and driving customer loyalty," she began. "We need to exceed our customers' expectations and demonstrate our commitment to their success."

David, the analytical thinker, nodded in agreement. "Effective post-sale follow-up requires proactive communication, ongoing support, and a focus on delivering value," he remarked. "We need to ensure a smooth transition from sale to implementation and beyond."

Emma, the strategist, interjected with enthusiasm. "Let's start by exploring post-sale follow-up strategies," she suggested. "We need to prioritize customer satisfaction, gather feedback, and identify opportunities for upselling and cross-selling."

Lisa clicked her remote, and the projector displayed a list of key elements for successful post-sale follow-up. "We'll focus on six main aspects: onboarding and implementation support, customer feedback gathering, proactive communication, upselling and cross-selling opportunities, customer appreciation gestures, and ongoing relationship nurturing," she said. "Each element is crucial for building strong, long-lasting relationships with our customers."

Onboarding and Implementation Support

Emma highlighted the importance of onboarding and implementation support. "A smooth onboarding process sets the stage for a positive customer experience," she noted. "We need to provide clear guidance, training, and resources to help our customers get up and running quickly."

David suggested assigning a dedicated onboarding specialist. "Having a single point of contact for onboarding can streamline the process and provide personalized support," he said. "The specialist can guide the customer through setup, configuration, and initial use of our products or services."

Lisa emphasized the need for ongoing support. "Our support team should be readily available to answer questions, address concerns, and provide technical assistance," she remarked. "Proactive communication and responsive support will build trust and confidence in our brand."

Customer Feedback Gathering

Emma focused on the importance of gathering customer feedback. "Feedback is essential for understanding our customers' needs, preferences, and pain points," she said. "We should regularly solicit feedback through surveys, interviews, and other channels to identify areas for improvement."

David suggested using feedback to drive product or service enhancements. "We should analyze feedback data to identify trends and patterns," he noted. "Insights from customer feedback can inform product roadmap decisions and drive continuous improvement."

Lisa emphasized the need for action based on feedback. "When customers provide feedback, they expect us to take action," she remarked. "We should communicate how we're addressing their feedback and demonstrate our commitment to their satisfaction."

Proactive Communication

Emma highlighted the importance of proactive communication. "Regular communication with our customers demonstrates our ongoing commitment to their success," she noted. "We should check in regularly, provide updates on new features or offerings, and offer proactive support."

David suggested using a multi-channel communication approach. "We should reach out to our customers through their preferred channels, whether it's email, phone, or social media," he said. "Personalized communication shows that we value their business and are invested in their success."

Lisa emphasized the need for personalized touchpoints. "Our communication should be tailored to each customer's needs and preferences," she remarked. "Personalization builds stronger connections and fosters a sense of loyalty."

Upselling and Cross-Selling Opportunities

Emma focused on the potential for upselling and cross-selling. "Existing customers are a valuable source of upsell and cross-sell opportunities," she said. "We should identify additional products or services that complement their existing purchase and present them as solutions to their evolving needs."

David suggested using data-driven insights for targeted offers. "We can analyze customer purchase history, behavior, and preferences to identify relevant upsell and cross-sell opportunities," he noted. "Targeted offers are more likely to resonate and drive conversion."

Lisa emphasized the need for value-driven messaging. "When presenting upsell or cross-sell opportunities, we should focus on the value they provide to the customer," she remarked. "Highlighting benefits and addressing pain points increases the likelihood of success."

Customer Appreciation Gestures

Emma highlighted the importance of showing appreciation to customers. "Customer appreciation gestures can strengthen our relationships and foster loyalty," she noted. "We should express gratitude through personalized messages, exclusive offers, or special events."

David suggested celebrating milestones with customers. "When customers reach significant milestones, such as anniversaries or achievements, we should celebrate with them," he said. "Recognition and appreciation reinforce their value to our business."

Lisa emphasized the need for authenticity in appreciation gestures. "Our gestures should be genuine and meaningful," she remarked. "Customers can tell when appreciation is sincere, and it strengthens the bond between us."

Ongoing Relationship Nurturing

Emma focused on the importance of ongoing relationship nurturing. "Building strong, long-lasting relationships requires ongoing effort and investment," she said. "We should continue to engage with our customers, provide value, and seek opportunities to deepen our connections."

David suggested creating a customer loyalty program. "A loyalty program rewards customers for their continued support and encourages repeat business," he noted. "We can offer exclusive benefits, discounts, or rewards to incentivize loyalty."

Lisa emphasized the need for proactive relationship management. "We should regularly reach out to our customers to check in, gather feedback, and offer support," she remarked. "Proactive communication strengthens our relationships and ensures customer satisfaction."

As they outlined their post-sale follow-up strategies, the team felt a renewed sense of commitment to their customers' success. They understood that by prioritizing customer satisfaction, gathering feedback, and nurturing relationships, they could build a loyal customer base and drive sustainable growth for InnovateTech.

Emma emphasized the importance of continuous improvement. "We need to regularly review and refine our post-sale follow-up strategies," she remarked. "By gathering feedback and analyzing performance, we can identify areas for improvement and ensure our approaches remain effective."

David suggested using analytics to track key metrics. "We need to monitor metrics such as customer satisfaction scores, retention rates, and upsell/cross-sell conversion rates," he said. "Regular analysis will help us refine our strategies and achieve better results."

With their post-sale follow-up strategies defined, the team felt a renewed sense of purpose. They knew that by prioritizing customer satisfaction and nurturing relationships, they could build a loyal customer base and drive sustainable growth for InnovateTech.

As they left the conference room, Emma, David, Lisa, and the rest of the team felt a sense of determination and excitement. They understood that by creating a powerful sales strategy with effective post-sale follow-up, they could propel InnovateTech towards greater success. Together, they would embark on a journey where every interaction with a customer echoed their brand narrative, guiding their customers towards shared prosperity and building lasting relationships with InnovateTech.

7

Chapter 7: Aligning Sales and Marketing Teams

Fostering Open Communication

In the heart of InnovateTech's headquarters, the leadership team gathered once more, this time to delve into the critical aspect of aligning sales and marketing teams. Emma, David, Lisa, and their colleagues recognized that effective collaboration between these two departments was essential for driving growth and delivering a seamless customer experience.

Lisa, the CEO, set the tone for the discussion with a determined tone. "Aligning our sales and marketing teams is crucial for maximizing our efforts and achieving our goals," she began. "We need to foster open communication, mutual respect, and shared objectives to ensure synergy between these two key functions."

David, the analytical thinker, nodded in agreement. "Effective communication is the cornerstone of successful collaboration between sales and marketing," he remarked. "We need to break down silos, encourage information sharing, and align our strategies to deliver a unified message to our customers."

Emma, the strategist, interjected with enthusiasm. "Let's start by exploring how we can foster open communication between our sales and marketing teams," she suggested. "We need to create opportunities for collaboration, establish clear channels of communication, and cultivate a culture of transparency and trust."

Lisa clicked her remote, and the projector displayed a list of key elements for fostering open communication between sales and marketing teams. "We'll focus on six main aspects: regular meetings and collaboration sessions, shared goals and KPIs, transparent communication channels, feedback mechanisms, cross-functional training and workshops, and leadership support," she said. "Each element is crucial for building a strong foundation of collaboration and alignment between our teams."

Regular Meetings and Collaboration Sessions

Emma highlighted the importance of regular meetings and collaboration sessions. "Scheduled meetings and collaboration sessions provide opportunities for our sales and marketing teams to come together, share insights, and align strategies," she noted. "We should establish a cadence for these meetings to ensure consistent communication and collaboration."

David suggested creating cross-functional project teams. "By bringing together representatives from both sales and marketing, we can foster collaboration and innovation," he said. "Project teams can work together to tackle specific initiatives or campaigns, leveraging the unique expertise of each department."

Lisa emphasized the need for active participation. "Attendance and engagement in meetings and collaboration sessions should be encouraged and incentivized," she remarked. "Active participation fosters a sense of ownership and accountability, driving greater alignment and collaboration."

Shared Goals and KPIs

Emma focused on the importance of shared goals and KPIs. "Aligning our sales and marketing teams requires a shared understanding of our objectives and how each team contributes to achieving them," she said. "We should establish common goals and KPIs that reflect our overarching business objectives."

David suggested creating a shared dashboard for tracking progress. "A shared dashboard allows our sales and marketing teams to monitor performance, track KPIs, and identify areas for improvement in real-time," he noted. "Transparency and visibility drive accountability and alignment."

Lisa emphasized the need for regular review and recalibration. "We should regularly review our goals and KPIs to ensure they remain relevant and achievable," she remarked. "Feedback from both sales and marketing teams should inform adjustments and refinements to our objectives."

Transparent Communication Channels

Emma highlighted the importance of transparent communication channels. "Effective communication requires clear and accessible channels for sharing information, updates, and feedback," she noted. "We should establish communication protocols and tools that facilitate seamless collaboration between our teams."

David suggested using technology to enhance communication. "Collaboration tools such as shared workspaces, messaging platforms, and project management software can streamline communication and facilitate information sharing," he said. "We should leverage technology to break down communication barriers and foster collaboration."

Lisa emphasized the need for open-door policies. "Leadership should encourage an open-door policy that welcomes feedback, questions, and concerns from both sales and marketing teams," she remarked. "Accessibility and approachability from leadership build trust and encourage open communication."

Feedback Mechanisms

Emma focused on the importance of feedback mechanisms. "Feedback is essential for continuous improvement and alignment between sales and marketing," she said. "We should establish formal feedback mechanisms, such as surveys, focus groups, and regular check-ins, to gather insights from both teams."

David suggested creating cross-functional feedback loops. "We should encourage sales and marketing teams to provide feedback to each other on campaigns, initiatives, and processes," he noted. "Cross-functional feedback fosters mutual understanding and drives collaboration."

Lisa emphasized the need for action based on feedback. "Feedback without action is meaningless," she remarked. "We should communicate how we're addressing feedback and implementing changes based on input from both sales and marketing teams."

Cross-Functional Training and Workshops

Emma highlighted the importance of cross-functional training and workshops. "Cross-functional training allows our sales and marketing teams to gain a deeper understanding of each other's roles, responsibilities, and challenges," she noted. "Workshops and training sessions provide opportunities for skill development, knowledge sharing, and relationship building."

David suggested creating role-playing exercises. "Role-playing exercises can simulate real-life scenarios and help sales and marketing teams understand each other's perspectives," he said. "By stepping into each other's shoes, team members gain empathy and insight, fostering collaboration and alignment."

Lisa emphasized the value of cross-departmental mentorship programs. "Pairing team members from sales and marketing for mentorship can foster mutual learning and support," she remarked. "Mentorship programs build relationships, facilitate knowledge transfer, and drive collaboration."

Leadership Support

Emma focused on the importance of leadership support. "Alignment between sales and marketing starts at the top," she said. "Leadership should demonstrate a commitment to collaboration, provide resources and support, and lead by example in fostering open communication and alignment between teams." David suggested creating cross-functional leadership teams.

Joint Planning Sessions

In the bustling conference room of InnovateTech's headquarters, the leadership team reconvened, eager to explore the next vital aspect of aligning sales and marketing teams: joint planning sessions. Emma, David, Lisa, and their colleagues understood that these sessions were pivotal for fostering collaboration, ensuring strategic alignment, and driving mutual success.

Lisa, the CEO, kicked off the discussion with her characteristic determination. "Joint planning sessions are the cornerstone of our efforts to align sales and marketing," she declared. "They provide a dedicated space for both teams to come together, align their strategies, and set shared objectives."

David, the analytical thinker, nodded in agreement. "Effective joint planning sessions enable us to leverage the strengths of both sales and marketing, identify synergies, and develop integrated strategies that resonate with our target audience," he remarked. "We need to ensure these sessions are productive, collaborative, and outcome-focused."

Emma, the strategist, interjected with enthusiasm. "Let's dive into how we can make our joint planning sessions impactful and beneficial for both teams," she suggested. "We need to establish clear objectives, facilitate open discussion, and empower teams to contribute their insights and expertise."

Lisa clicked her remote, and the projector displayed a list of key elements for successful joint planning sessions between sales and marketing teams. "We'll focus on six main aspects: setting clear objectives and agendas, fostering open dialogue and collaboration, aligning strategies and priorities, identifying opportunities for integration, assigning ownership and accountability, and evaluating outcomes and refining strategies," she said. "Each element is crucial for driving alignment and synergy between our teams."

Setting Clear Objectives and Agendas

Emma emphasized the importance of setting clear objectives and agendas for joint planning sessions. "Clear objectives provide focus and direction, ensuring that our discussions are productive and outcome-oriented," she noted. "We should establish specific goals for each session and develop agendas that outline key topics, discussion points, and desired outcomes."

David suggested soliciting input from both sales and marketing teams when setting objectives and agendas. "By involving team members in the planning process, we can ensure that our sessions address their needs, priorities, and challenges," he remarked. "This fosters ownership and engagement, driving more meaningful discussions and outcomes."

Lisa emphasized the need for flexibility in agendas. "While

it's essential to have a structured agenda, we should also allow for flexibility to address emergent topics or opportunities," she said. "Agendas should be dynamic documents that evolve based on the needs and priorities of our teams."

Fostering Open Dialogue and Collaboration

Emma highlighted the importance of fostering open dialogue and collaboration during joint planning sessions. "Open dialogue creates a space for teams to share insights, ideas, and feedback openly," she noted. "We should encourage active participation, respectful communication, and constructive debate to drive collaboration and innovation."

David suggested using facilitators to guide discussions and ensure equitable participation. "Facilitators can help keep discussions on track, manage time effectively, and encourage contributions from all team members," he said. "They can also help navigate conflicts or disagreements and ensure that everyone's perspectives are heard and valued."

Lisa emphasized the need for inclusivity. "Our joint planning sessions should be inclusive, welcoming diverse perspectives and contributions from all team members," she remarked. "We should create a culture where everyone feels empowered to speak up, share their ideas, and challenge assumptions."

Aligning Strategies and Priorities

Emma focused on the importance of aligning strategies and priorities during joint planning sessions. "Alignment ensures that our sales and marketing teams are working towards common goals and objectives," she said. "We should review our respective strategies, identify areas of alignment or divergence, and develop integrated plans that leverage the strengths of both teams."

David suggested conducting SWOT analyses to identify opportunities for integration and alignment. "SWOT analyses allow us to assess our strengths, weaknesses, opportunities, and threats as a combined sales and marketing organization," he noted. "They help us identify synergies, gaps, and areas for improvement, informing our strategic planning and decision-making."

Lisa emphasized the need for compromise and collaboration when aligning strategies. "Alignment requires flexibility and a willingness to compromise," she remarked. "We should seek common ground, find win-win solutions, and prioritize the collective success of our organization over individual interests."

Identifying Opportunities for Integration

Emma highlighted the importance of identifying opportunities for integration during joint planning sessions. "Integration allows us to leverage the strengths of both sales and marketing to deliver a unified customer experience," she noted. "We should identify touchpoints and handoffs between our teams, streamline processes, and develop integrated campaigns and initiatives that span the entire customer journey."

David suggested creating cross-functional project teams to drive integration efforts. "Cross-functional project teams bring together representatives from sales, marketing, and other relevant departments to collaborate on specific initiatives or campaigns," he said. "They ensure alignment, accountability, and shared ownership, driving more cohesive and effective outcomes."

Lisa emphasized the value of data-driven decision-making in identifying integration opportunities. "Data provides valuable insights into customer behavior, preferences, and engagement," she remarked. "We should analyze data from both sales and marketing to identify areas of synergy and opportunities for integration, informing our joint planning efforts."

Assigning Ownership and Accountability

Emma focused on the importance of assigning ownership and accountability during joint planning sessions. "Clear ownership ensures that initiatives and actions are executed effectively and efficiently," she said. "We should assign responsibilities, establish timelines, and define success metrics to drive accountability and track progress."

David suggested creating cross-functional teams to oversee key initiatives or campaigns. "Cross-functional teams bring together representatives from sales, marketing, and other relevant departments to collaborate on specific projects or campaigns," he noted. "They ensure alignment, coordination, and accountability, driving more effective execution and results."

Lisa emphasized the need for regular check-ins and progress reviews. "We should schedule regular check-ins to monitor progress, address challenges, and celebrate successes," she remarked. "Transparent communication and accountability drive momentum and ensure that our initiatives stay on track."

Evaluating Outcomes and Refining Strategies

Emma highlighted the importance of evaluating outcomes and refining strategies based on joint planning sessions. "Evaluation allows us to assess the effectiveness of our initiatives, identify lessons learned, and make data-driven adjustments," she noted. "We should review outcomes against our objectives, gather feedback from stakeholders, and iterate on our strategies to drive continuous improvement."

David suggested using post-mortem reviews to assess outcomes and identify areas for improvement.

Shared Metrics and KPIs

In the boardroom of InnovateTech's headquarters, the leadership team gathered once more, this time to explore the critical aspect of establishing shared metrics and key performance indicators (KPIs) between the sales and marketing teams. Emma, David, Lisa, and their colleagues understood that aligning these metrics was essential for fostering collaboration, driving accountability, and measuring the success of their joint efforts.

Lisa, the CEO, set the tone for the discussion with her characteristic determination. "Establishing shared metrics and KPIs between sales and marketing is vital for ensuring that both teams are working towards common goals and objectives," she declared. "We need to identify metrics that reflect our overarching business objectives and align with the entire customer journey."

David, the analytical thinker, nodded in agreement. "Shared metrics and KPIs provide a unified framework for measuring performance and driving alignment between sales and marketing," he remarked. "We need to ensure that these metrics are meaningful, actionable, and reflective of our collective efforts."

Emma, the strategist, interjected with enthusiasm. "Let's dive into how we can establish shared metrics and KPIs that drive alignment and collaboration between our teams," she suggested. "We need to define clear metrics, establish benchmarks, and regularly review performance to drive continuous improvement."

Lisa clicked her remote, and the projector displayed a list of key elements for establishing shared metrics and KPIs between sales and marketing teams. "We'll focus on six main aspects: defining common objectives, selecting relevant metrics, establishing benchmarks and targets, integrating data and reporting systems, fostering transparency and accountability, and iterating based on feedback and performance," she said. "Each element is crucial for driving alignment and synergy between our teams."

Defining Common Objectives

Emma emphasized the importance of defining common objectives to drive alignment between sales and marketing teams. "Common objectives provide a shared purpose and direction for both teams," she noted. "We should align our objectives with the overall business goals, such as revenue growth, customer acquisition, or market expansion."

David suggested involving both sales and marketing teams in the objective-setting process. "By soliciting input from both teams, we can ensure that our objectives are realistic, achievable, and meaningful to everyone," he remarked. "This fosters ownership and commitment, driving greater alignment and collaboration."

Lisa emphasized the need for clarity and specificity in objectives. "Our objectives should be clear, specific, and measurable," she said. "They should outline what we want to achieve, by when, and how we'll measure success, providing a framework for aligning our efforts and tracking our progress."

Selecting Relevant Metrics

Emma focused on the importance of selecting relevant metrics to measure the success of sales and marketing efforts. "Relevant metrics provide insights into the effectiveness of our strategies and tactics," she noted. "We should identify metrics that align with our objectives and reflect the entire customer journey, from awareness to conversion."

David suggested using a balanced mix of leading and lagging indicators. "Leading indicators provide early signals of performance trends, while lagging indicators measure outcomes or results," he explained. "We should use a combination of both types of metrics to provide a comprehensive view of our performance."

Lisa emphasized the need for alignment between sales and marketing metrics. "Our metrics should be aligned across sales and marketing teams to ensure consistency and comparability," she remarked. "This allows us to identify areas of synergy, measure the impact of our joint efforts, and drive alignment between teams."

Establishing Benchmarks and Targets

Emma highlighted the importance of establishing benchmarks and targets to measure progress and drive performance improvement. "Benchmarks provide context for interpreting our performance and comparing it to industry standards or historical data," she noted. "Targets set clear expectations and provide motivation for achieving our goals."

David suggested using SMART criteria to set targets. "SMART criteria ensure that our targets are specific, measurable, achievable, relevant, and time-bound," he explained. "This provides clarity and focus, guiding our efforts towards meaningful outcomes."

Lisa emphasized the need for flexibility in targets. "While targets provide a goal to strive for, we should also allow for flexibility to adapt to changing market conditions or business priorities," she remarked. "Targets should be periodically reviewed and adjusted based on performance and external factors."

Integrating Data and Reporting Systems

Emma focused on the importance of integrating data and reporting systems to ensure consistency and accuracy in performance measurement. "Integrated data and reporting systems provide a single source of truth for sales and marketing metrics," she noted. "We should integrate our CRM, marketing automation, and analytics platforms to streamline data collection and reporting."

David suggested establishing data governance policies to ensure data quality and integrity. "Data governance policies define standards and procedures for data collection, storage, and usage," he explained. "They ensure that our data is accurate, reliable, and compliant with regulatory requirements."

Lisa emphasized the need for transparency and accessibility in reporting systems. "Our reporting systems should be transparent and accessible to all team members," she remarked. "This fosters accountability and empowers team members to track their performance, identify areas for improvement, and drive continuous growth."

Fostering Transparency and Accountability

Emma highlighted the importance of fostering transparency and accountability in measuring and reporting performance. "Transparency builds trust and credibility, ensuring that our teams have visibility into each other's efforts and contributions," she noted. "Accountability drives ownership and responsibility, motivating team members to strive for excellence."

David suggested creating dashboards or scorecards to visualize performance metrics and track progress towards targets. "Dashboards provide a visual representation of our performance metrics, allowing team members to quickly assess their progress and identify areas for improvement," he said. "They serve as a powerful tool for fostering transparency and accountability."

Lisa emphasized the need for regular performance reviews and feedback sessions. "We should schedule regular performance reviews to discuss progress towards targets, celebrate successes, and address challenges," she remarked. "Feedback sessions provide opportunities for coaching, mentoring, and professional development, driving continuous improvement and growth."

Iterating Based on Feedback and Performance

Emma focused on the importance of iterating based on feedback and performance to drive continuous improvement. "Feedback provides valuable insights into our performance and areas for improvement," she noted. "We should regularly review our performance metrics, gather feedback from stakeholders, and iterate on our strategies and tactics to drive continuous growth."

David suggested using agile methodologies to iterate quickly and adapt to changing market dynamics. "

Regular Feedback Loops

As the sunlight streamed through the windows of the boardroom at InnovateTech, the leadership team gathered once more, this time to discuss the importance of establishing regular feedback loops between the sales and marketing teams. Emma, David, Lisa, and their colleagues understood that fostering open communication and continuous improvement relied heavily on the exchange of feedback.

Lisa, the CEO, set the stage for the discussion with her characteristic clarity. "Regular feedback loops are crucial for ensuring that our sales and marketing efforts remain aligned, effective, and responsive to market dynamics," she declared. "We need to create structured channels for feedback exchange and cultivate a culture that values input from both teams."

David, the analytical thinker, nodded in agreement. "Feedback loops provide a mechanism for identifying strengths, weaknesses, and opportunities for improvement," he remarked. "We need to establish a feedback culture that encourages constructive criticism, active listening, and collaboration between sales and marketing."

Emma, the strategist, interjected with enthusiasm. "Let's explore how we can establish regular feedback loops that drive alignment and continuous improvement between our teams," she suggested. "We need to define clear feedback mechanisms, establish regular cadences for feedback exchange, and ensure that feedback is acted upon promptly."

Lisa clicked her remote, and the projector displayed a list of key elements for establishing regular feedback loops between sales and marketing teams. "We'll focus on six main aspects: creating structured feedback channels, establishing regular cadences for feedback exchange, promoting a culture of openness and receptiveness, acting on feedback promptly, fostering trust and transparency, and iterating based on feedback and performance," she said. "Each element is essential for driving alignment and synergy between our teams."

Creating Structured Feedback Channels

Emma emphasized the importance of creating structured feedback channels to facilitate the exchange of feedback between sales and marketing teams. "Structured channels provide a clear framework for soliciting, collecting, and managing feedback," she noted. "We should establish channels such as feedback forms, surveys, suggestion boxes, or regular feedback sessions to ensure that feedback is captured effectively."

David suggested leveraging technology to streamline feedback collection and management. "Technology solutions such as feedback management systems or collaboration platforms can automate the feedback collection process, centralize feedback data, and facilitate analysis and reporting," he explained. "This allows us to capture feedback in real-time and take action promptly."

Lisa emphasized the need for anonymity in feedback channels to encourage honest and candid input. "Anonymity ensures that team members feel comfortable providing feedback without fear of repercussions," she remarked. "We should offer anonymous feedback options to promote openness and transparency in our feedback culture."

Establishing Regular Cadences for Feedback Exchange

Emma focused on the importance of establishing regular cadences for feedback exchange between sales and marketing teams. "Regular feedback exchange ensures that feedback is timely, relevant, and actionable," she noted. "We should schedule recurring feedback sessions, check-ins, or reviews to facilitate ongoing dialogue and collaboration between teams."

David suggested aligning feedback cadences with key milestones or touchpoints in the sales and marketing processes. "Feedback sessions can be scheduled around key events such as campaign launches, sales meetings, or quarterly business reviews," he said. "This ensures that feedback is contextual and meaningful, driving more targeted and impactful improvements."

Lisa emphasized the need for consistency and predictability in feedback cadences. "Consistent feedback sessions help build trust and accountability," she remarked. "Team members know when to expect feedback sessions and can come prepared to share their insights, ideas, and concerns."

Promoting a Culture of Openness and Receptiveness

Emma highlighted the importance of promoting a culture of openness and receptiveness to feedback within sales and marketing teams. "A culture that values feedback encourages active participation, constructive dialogue, and continuous improvement," she noted. "We should create an environment where team members feel empowered to share their perspectives, challenge assumptions, and contribute to collective growth."

David suggested leading by example in promoting a feedback culture. "Leadership plays a crucial role in shaping organizational culture," he remarked. "Leaders should demonstrate openness to feedback, actively solicit input from team members, and respond constructively to feedback received."

Lisa emphasized the need for active listening in fostering a feedback culture. "Active listening involves not only hearing feedback but also understanding, empathizing, and responding to it," she said. "We should encourage team members to listen actively, ask clarifying questions, and seek to understand different perspectives."

Acting on Feedback Promptly

Emma focused on the importance of acting on feedback promptly to demonstrate responsiveness and commitment to continuous improvement. "Prompt action on feedback shows that we value input from our team members and are committed to addressing their concerns and suggestions," she noted. "We should prioritize feedback that has the greatest potential to drive positive change and take action to implement relevant improvements."

David suggested establishing clear processes for reviewing and acting on feedback. "We should establish feedback review committees or designated individuals responsible for reviewing feedback, identifying actionable insights, and prioritizing improvement initiatives," he said. "Clear processes ensure that feedback is not only collected but also acted upon effectively."

Lisa emphasized the need for transparency in communicating actions taken in response to feedback. "Transparency builds trust and credibility," she remarked. "We should communicate openly with our team members about the actions taken in response to their feedback, the rationale behind those actions, and the expected outcomes."

Fostering Trust and Transparency

Emma highlighted the importance of fostering trust and transparency in feedback exchange between sales and marketing teams. "Trust is the foundation of effective feedback exchange," she noted. "We should create an environment where team members feel comfortable sharing their feedback, knowing that it will be received respectfully, considered thoughtfully, and acted upon promptly."

David suggested creating feedback champions or advocates within sales and marketing teams to promote trust and transparency. "Feedback champions can serve as ambassadors for feedback culture, advocating for its importance, facilitating feedback exchange, and promoting transparency in feedback processes," he explained. "They can also serve as liaisons between teams, ensuring that feedback is effectively communicated and addressed."

Lisa emphasized the need for transparency in feedback processes and outcomes. "Transparency builds credibility and confidence in feedback processes," she remarked. "We should be transparent about how feedback is collected, reviewed, and acted upon, as well as the outcomes and impacts of feedback-driven initiatives."

Iterating Based on Feedback and Performance

Emma focused on the importance of iterating based on feedback and performance to drive continuous improvement. "Feedback provides valuable insights into our performance and areas for improvement," she noted. "We should regularly review our feedback processes, gather input from team members, and iterate on our approaches to foster continuous improvement and growth." David suggested using agile methodologies to iterate quickly and adapt to changing needs and preferences. "

Conflict Resolution Strategies

As the day waned and shadows danced across the boardroom of InnovateTech, the leadership team convened once more, this time to delve into the delicate yet essential topic of conflict resolution strategies between the sales and marketing teams. Emma, David, Lisa, and their colleagues knew that in the pursuit of alignment, conflicts were inevitable, but how they

CHAPTER 7: ALIGNING SALES AND MARKETING TEAMS

were addressed could make all the difference.

Lisa, the CEO, began with a tone of diplomacy. "Conflict is a natural part of collaboration, but how we handle it determines our success," she stated. "We need effective conflict resolution strategies to address disputes, promote understanding, and maintain harmony between our sales and marketing teams."

David, the analytical mind, nodded, recognizing the importance of structured conflict resolution. "Addressing conflicts promptly and constructively prevents escalation and fosters a culture of collaboration," he commented. "We need strategies that encourage open communication, empathy, and compromise."

Emma, the strategic thinker, interjected with a thoughtful perspective. "Let's explore how we can navigate conflicts between our sales and marketing teams with grace and effectiveness," she proposed. "We need to establish clear processes, foster empathy, and focus on finding win-win solutions that benefit both teams."

Lisa clicked her remote, and the projector displayed a list of key elements for conflict resolution strategies between sales and marketing teams. "We'll focus on six main aspects: establishing clear processes for conflict resolution, fostering open communication and active listening, promoting empathy and understanding, focusing on interests rather than positions, seeking win-win solutions, and following up to ensure resolution and prevent recurrence," she explained. "Each element is crucial for maintaining collaboration and alignment between our teams."

Establishing Clear Processes for Conflict Resolution

Emma emphasized the importance of having clear processes for conflict resolution in place. "Clear processes provide a structured framework for addressing conflicts, ensuring that they are resolved promptly and fairly," she noted. "We should establish clear escalation paths, designate points of contact, and define roles and responsibilities for managing conflicts between sales and marketing teams."

David suggested creating a conflict resolution playbook. "A conflict resolution playbook outlines step-by-step procedures for addressing different types of conflicts," he explained. "It provides guidance on how to identify, assess, and resolve conflicts effectively, empowering team members to navigate challenging situations with confidence."

Lisa emphasized the need for transparency in conflict resolution processes. "Transparency builds trust and confidence in conflict resolution processes," she remarked. "We should communicate openly with our teams about how conflicts are addressed, the expected timelines for resolution, and the available resources and support."

Fostering Open Communication and Active Listening

Emma highlighted the importance of fostering open communication and active listening in resolving conflicts between sales and marketing teams. "Open communication creates a safe space for team members to express their concerns, share their perspectives, and work towards resolution," she noted. "We should encourage active listening, empathy, and respect for diverse viewpoints."

David suggested using techniques such as reflective listening to enhance understanding and empathy. "Reflective listening involves paraphrasing and summarizing the speaker's message to demonstrate understanding and validate their feelings," he explained. "It fosters empathy and trust, paving the way for constructive dialogue and resolution."

Lisa emphasized the need for empathy in conflict resolution. "Empathy involves understanding and acknowledging the emotions and perspectives of others," she remarked. "We should encourage team members to put themselves in each other's shoes, consider the impact of their actions and words, and approach conflicts with compassion and understanding."

Promoting Empathy and Understanding

Emma focused on the importance of promoting empathy and understanding in resolving conflicts between sales and marketing teams. "Empathy fosters mutual respect, trust, and collaboration," she noted. "We should encourage team members to listen actively, acknowledge each other's perspectives, and seek common ground to resolve conflicts effectively."

David suggested using role-playing exercises to cultivate empathy and understanding. "Role-playing exercises allow team members to step into each other's shoes and experience different perspectives firsthand," he explained. "They promote empathy, perspective-taking, and insight, facilitating more constructive and empathetic communication."

Lisa emphasized the need for patience and tolerance in conflict resolution. "Resolving conflicts takes time and effort," she remarked. "We should be patient, tolerant, and respectful towards each other, even when tensions run high, recognizing that conflicts are opportunities for growth and learning."

Focusing on Interests Rather than Positions

Emma highlighted the importance of focusing on interests rather than positions in resolving conflicts between sales and marketing teams. "Interests represent the underlying needs, concerns, and priorities driving each party's position in a conflict," she noted. "We should encourage team members to identify their interests, communicate them openly, and explore creative solutions that address the interests of all parties."

David suggested using interest-based negotiation techniques to find mutually beneficial solutions. "Interest-based negotiation focuses on identifying shared interests, exploring options for meeting those interests, and finding win-win solutions," he explained. "It promotes collaboration, innovation, and relationship-building, fostering stronger alignment between sales and marketing teams."

Lisa emphasized the need for flexibility and creativity in conflict resolution. "Flexible and creative solutions often arise when we focus on interests rather than positions," she remarked. "We should be open to exploring different options, thinking outside the box, and finding innovative solutions that meet the needs of all parties involved."

Seeking Win-Win Solutions

Emma focused on the importance of seeking win-win solutions in resolving conflicts between sales and marketing teams. "Win-win solutions ensure that both parties' interests are addressed and that the outcome is mutually beneficial," she noted. "We should collaborate creatively, brainstorm options, and negotiate in good faith to find solutions that satisfy the needs of both teams."

David suggested using collaborative problem-solving techniques to generate win-win solutions. "Collaborative problem-solving involves brainstorming, exploring alternatives, and evaluating options together," he explained. "It encourages teamwork, creativity, and shared ownership, leading to more sustainable and satisfactory outcomes."

Lisa emphasized the need for compromise and flexibility in conflict resolution. "Compromise involves making concessions and finding middle ground to resolve conflicts," she remarked. "We should be willing to compromise on certain issues, prioritize our common goals and interests, and focus on achieving a resolution that benefits both teams."

Following Up to Ensure Resolution and Prevent Recurrence

Emma highlighted the importance of following up to ensure resolution and prevent recurrence of conflicts between sales and marketing teams. "Following up demonstrates our commitment to addressing conflicts effectively and preventing their recurrence," she noted. "We should check in with the involved parties, gather feedback on the effectiveness of the resolution, and take proactive steps to address any underlying issues or systemic causes."

David suggested using post-mortem reviews to assess the effectiveness of conflict resolution efforts and identify areas for improvement. "Post-mortem reviews involve reflecting on the conflict resolution process, analyzing what worked well and what could be improved, and identifying lessons learned," he explained. "They help us refine our conflict resolution strategies and build organizational resilience."

Celebrating Joint Successes

As the sun set beyond the windows of InnovateTech's boardroom, the leadership team reconvened, this time to discuss the significance of celebrating joint successes between the sales and marketing teams. Emma, David, Lisa, and their colleagues understood that recognizing shared achievements was essential for fostering camaraderie, boosting morale, and reinforcing collaboration.

Lisa, the CEO, initiated the conversation with a warm smile. "Celebrating our joint successes is not just about acknowledging achievements; it's about reinforcing our unity and collective efforts," she stated. "We need to create a culture where we celebrate wins together, regardless of which team they originate from."

David, the analytical thinker, nodded in agreement. "Celebrating joint successes strengthens our bond as a unified team," he remarked. "It's a powerful way to recognize the contributions of both sales and marketing teams, build camaraderie, and motivate everyone to continue working towards our shared goals."

Emma, the strategist, interjected with enthusiasm. "Let's explore how we can celebrate our joint successes in meaningful and memorable ways," she suggested. "We need to create rituals, events, and traditions that bring our teams together, celebrate achievements, and reinforce our shared purpose and values."

Lisa clicked her remote, and the projector displayed a list of key elements for celebrating joint successes between sales and marketing teams. "We'll focus on six main aspects: creating a culture of celebration, recognizing individual and team achievements, sharing success stories, organizing joint events and activities, expressing gratitude and appreciation, and leveraging technology to amplify celebrations," she explained. "Each element is crucial for fostering collaboration and alignment between our teams."

Creating a Culture of Celebration

Emma emphasized the importance of creating a culture of celebration within the organization. "A culture of celebration fosters positivity, camaraderie, and morale," she noted. "We should celebrate not only major milestones but also small wins and achievements along the way, recognizing the efforts and contributions of our teams."

David suggested establishing rituals or traditions to mark successes. "Rituals provide a sense of continuity and belonging," he explained. "We should establish traditions such as weekly shout-outs, monthly celebrations, or quarterly awards ceremonies to recognize and celebrate achievements consistently."

Lisa emphasized the need for leadership involvement in celebrating successes. "Leadership sets the tone for organizational culture," she remarked. "We should lead by example in celebrating successes, expressing appreciation, and reinforcing our values of collaboration and teamwork."

Recognizing Individual and Team Achievements

Emma highlighted the importance of recognizing both individual and team achievements. "Recognition is a powerful motivator that drives engagement and performance," she noted. "We should celebrate the accomplishments of individual team members as well as the collective achievements of our sales and marketing teams."

David suggested using a variety of recognition methods to appeal to different preferences and personalities. "Recognition can take many forms, from public praise and awards to private acknowledgments and incentives," he explained. "We should tailor our recognition efforts to individual preferences, ensuring that everyone feels valued and appreciated."

Lisa emphasized the need for sincerity and specificity in recognition. "Sincere recognition is meaningful and impactful," she remarked. "We should be specific in our praise, highlighting the actions, behaviors, or results that led to success and expressing genuine appreciation for the efforts of our team members."

Sharing Success Stories

Emma focused on the importance of sharing success stories to inspire and motivate the team. "Success stories provide tangible examples of what's possible when we work together towards a common goal," she noted. "We should share stories of collaboration, innovation, and achievement to celebrate our successes and reinforce our shared purpose and values."

David suggested creating a platform or channel for sharing success stories. "A dedicated platform, such as a newsletter, blog, or social media page, allows us to showcase success stories and celebrate achievements with a wider audience," he explained. "It creates visibility and recognition for our teams' efforts and accomplishments."

Lisa emphasized the need for authenticity and inclusivity in sharing success stories. "Success stories should be authentic and relatable," she remarked. "We should highlight a diverse range of achievements and contributions from across our sales and marketing teams, ensuring that everyone feels included and valued."

Organizing Joint Events and Activities

Emma highlighted the importance of organizing joint events and activities to celebrate successes and build camaraderie between sales and marketing teams. "Joint events provide opportunities for team members to come together, bond, and celebrate their achievements in a fun and relaxed environment," she noted. "We should organize events such as team outings, offsite retreats, or themed parties to celebrate our joint successes."

David suggested involving both sales and marketing teams in event planning to ensure inclusivity and engagement. "Event planning committees can include representatives from both teams to brainstorm ideas, coordinate logistics, and ensure that events reflect the interests and preferences of all team members," he explained. "This promotes ownership, participation, and buy-in from both teams."

Lisa emphasized the need for variety and creativity in event planning.

8

Chapter 8: Leveraging Data and Analytics

Importance of Data-Driven Decision Making

The morning sun illuminated the sleek, modern office of InnovateTech as the leadership team assembled for a critical discussion on the future of their business. The atmosphere buzzed with anticipation as Lisa, Emma, David, and their colleagues took their seats around the conference table, prepared to delve into the importance of data-driven decision-making.

Lisa, the CEO, began the meeting with a sense of urgency and determination. "In today's fast-paced and competitive market, relying on gut feelings and intuition is no longer sufficient," she declared. "To stay ahead, we need to make informed decisions based on accurate and comprehensive data."

David, the analytical mind, nodded in agreement, his eyes gleaming with the excitement of the data-driven possibilities.

"Data-driven decision-making allows us to identify trends, uncover insights, and make strategic choices that drive growth and efficiency," he remarked. "We need to leverage data and analytics to make more informed and effective decisions across all aspects of our business."

Emma, the strategist, interjected with a thoughtful tone. "Let's explore how data-driven decision-making can transform our approach and propel us towards greater success," she suggested. "We need to understand the importance of data, establish robust data collection and analysis processes, and foster a culture that values and relies on data for decision-making."

Lisa clicked her remote, and the projector displayed a series of slides outlining the key elements of data-driven decision-making. "We'll focus on six main aspects: understanding the value of data, establishing data collection and management processes, leveraging advanced analytics, fostering a data-driven culture, integrating data into decision-making processes, and continuously improving through data insights," she explained. "Each element is crucial for harnessing the power of data and analytics to drive our business forward."

Understanding the Value of Data

Emma emphasized the foundational importance of recognizing the value of data. "Data is one of our most valuable assets," she noted. "It provides insights into customer behavior, market trends, operational efficiency, and financial performance. We need to treat data with the same importance as any other strategic asset."

David suggested conducting a data audit to identify and

evaluate the existing data sources within the organization. "A data audit helps us understand the types of data we have, their quality, and their potential applications," he explained. "It allows us to identify gaps, redundancies, and opportunities for data integration and optimization."

Lisa emphasized the need for data literacy across the organization. "Data literacy involves understanding how to interpret, analyze, and use data effectively," she remarked. "We should invest in training and development programs to enhance data literacy among our team members, ensuring that everyone can contribute to data-driven decision-making."

Establishing Data Collection and Management Processes

Emma highlighted the importance of establishing robust data collection and management processes. "Effective data collection and management are critical for ensuring that we have accurate, reliable, and timely data for decision-making," she noted. "We need to implement standardized processes for data collection, storage, and maintenance."

David suggested using automated tools and technologies to streamline data collection and management. "Automation reduces the risk of human error, enhances data accuracy, and improves efficiency," he explained. "We should leverage data management platforms, data warehousing solutions, and data integration tools to ensure that our data is consistent and accessible."

Lisa emphasized the need for data governance policies to ensure data quality and compliance. "Data governance policies define standards and procedures for data management, ensuring that our data is accurate, secure, and compliant with regulatory requirements," she remarked. "We should establish data governance committees or roles responsible for overseeing data quality and integrity."

Leveraging Advanced Analytics

Emma focused on the importance of leveraging advanced analytics to gain deeper insights from data. "Advanced analytics techniques, such as predictive analytics, machine learning, and artificial intelligence, allow us to uncover patterns, predict outcomes, and make more informed decisions," she noted. "We need to invest in advanced analytics capabilities to stay ahead of the competition."

David suggested partnering with external experts or consultants to enhance our analytics capabilities. "External experts bring specialized knowledge and experience that can help us implement advanced analytics solutions effectively," he explained. "They can also provide training and support to build our internal analytics capabilities."

Lisa emphasized the need for a strategic approach to analytics. "Analytics should be aligned with our business objectives and priorities," she remarked. "We should define clear analytics goals, identify key performance indicators (KPIs), and establish processes for monitoring and evaluating the impact of our analytics initiatives."

Fostering a Data-Driven Culture

Emma highlighted the importance of fostering a data-driven culture within the organization. "A data-driven culture values data as a critical asset and relies on data for decision-making," she noted. "We need to create an environment where data is accessible, data-driven decisions are encouraged, and data insights are celebrated."

David suggested promoting data-driven decision-making through leadership and communication. "Leaders play a crucial role in shaping organizational culture," he remarked. "We should lead by example, making data-driven decisions and communicating the importance of data to our teams."

Lisa emphasized the need for collaboration and knowledge sharing in fostering a data-driven culture. "Collaboration and knowledge sharing enhance our collective data capabilities," she explained. "We should encourage cross-functional teams to collaborate on data projects, share insights, and learn from each other's experiences."

Integrating Data into Decision-Making Processes

Emma focused on the importance of integrating data into decision-making processes across all levels of the organization. "Data should be an integral part of our decision-making processes, from strategic planning to daily operations," she noted. "We need to establish frameworks and tools that facilitate data-driven decision-making."

David suggested using decision support systems and dashboards to enhance data accessibility and visualization. "Decision support systems and dashboards provide real-time access to critical data and insights," he explained. "They enable us to make informed decisions quickly and effectively."

Lisa emphasized the need for alignment between data and business goals. "Our data initiatives should be aligned with our business goals and priorities," she remarked. "We should define clear objectives for our data projects and measure their impact on our overall performance."

Continuously Improving Through Data Insights

Emma highlighted the importance of continuously improving through data insights. "Data provides valuable feedback on our performance and areas for improvement," she noted. "We should regularly review our data, analyze trends, and use insights to drive continuous improvement and innovation."

David suggested implementing a cycle of data analysis, feedback, and action. "A continuous improvement cycle involves analyzing data, gathering feedback, and taking action to address identified issues or opportunities," he explained. "This iterative process ensures that we are constantly learning and evolving."

Lisa emphasized the need for agility and adaptability in leveraging data. "The business environment is constantly changing," she remarked. "We should be agile and adaptable, using data insights to respond to emerging trends, challenges, and opportunities effectively."

As the meeting concluded, the room was filled with a sense of optimism and determination. The leadership team at InnovateTech understood that leveraging data and analytics was not just a strategy, but a fundamental shift in how they operated and made decisions. With a clear vision and a commitment to data-driven decision-making, they were ready to navigate the future with confidence and insight.

Tools for Data Collection and Analysis

The boardroom at InnovateTech was alive with energy as the leadership team, led by Lisa, reconvened to discuss the essential tools for data collection and analysis. The focus was on selecting the right technologies to enable their transition to a data-driven organization. Emma, David, and their colleagues were eager to explore the possibilities that modern tools could bring to their decision-making processes.

Lisa started the meeting with an enthusiastic tone. "To harness the power of data, we need the right tools," she began. "These tools will help us collect, manage, and analyze data efficiently, providing us with actionable insights that drive our strategies forward."

David, the analytical mind, agreed. "The right tools can transform raw data into meaningful information," he remarked. "They can help us automate data collection, ensure data accuracy, and provide advanced analytical capabilities."

Emma, the strategist, leaned forward. "Let's dive into the specific tools we need and how they can benefit us," she suggested. "We need a comprehensive toolkit that covers data collection, storage, management, and analysis."

Lisa clicked her remote, and the projector displayed a list of essential tools for data collection and analysis. "We'll focus on six main categories: data collection tools, data management platforms, data warehousing solutions, analytics software, visualization tools, and machine learning platforms," she explained. "Each category plays a crucial role in our data ecosystem."

Data Collection Tools

Emma emphasized the importance of efficient data collection tools. "Data collection is the first step in our data journey," she noted. "We need tools that can gather data from various sources, including customer interactions, sales transactions, and marketing campaigns."

David suggested using web analytics tools like Google Analytics to track website traffic and user behavior. "Web analytics tools provide insights into how users interact with our website," he explained. "They help us understand user preferences, identify trends, and optimize our online presence."

Lisa highlighted the importance of customer relationship management (CRM) systems like Salesforce. "CRM systems centralize customer data and interactions," she remarked. "They provide a comprehensive view of customer behavior, preferences, and history, enabling personalized marketing and sales strategies."

Data Management Platforms

Emma focused on the need for robust data management platforms. "Data management platforms ensure that our data is organized, secure, and accessible," she noted. "We need tools that can handle large volumes of data, ensure data integrity, and support data integration."

David suggested using data integration tools like Talend or Informatica. "Data integration tools enable us to combine data from different sources," he explained. "They ensure that our data is consistent and accurate, providing a unified view of our information."

Lisa emphasized the importance of data governance solutions like Collibra. "Data governance solutions define standards and policies for data management," she remarked. "They ensure that our data is compliant with regulatory requirements and that we maintain high data quality."

Data Warehousing Solutions

Emma highlighted the role of data warehousing solutions in managing and storing data. "Data warehouses provide a centralized repository for our data," she noted. "They enable us to store, manage, and retrieve large volumes of data efficiently."

David suggested using cloud-based data warehousing solutions like Amazon Redshift or Google BigQuery. "Cloud-based solutions offer scalability and flexibility," he explained. "They allow us to handle growing data volumes and provide powerful querying capabilities."

Lisa emphasized the need for data lake solutions like Azure Data Lake for storing unstructured data. "Data lakes allow us to store raw, unstructured data," she remarked. "They enable us to capture diverse data types and support advanced analytics and machine learning."

Analytics Software

Emma focused on the importance of analytics software for gaining insights from data. "Analytics software enables us to analyze data, identify patterns, and make data-driven decisions," she noted. "We need tools that provide advanced analytical capabilities, including predictive and prescriptive analytics."

David suggested using business intelligence (BI) tools like Tableau or Power BI. "BI tools provide interactive dashboards and visualizations," he explained. "They help us explore data, create reports, and share insights with stakeholders."

Lisa highlighted the importance of statistical analysis software like R or SAS. "Statistical analysis software enables us to perform complex data analyses," she remarked. "They provide advanced statistical techniques and algorithms for in-depth data exploration."

Visualization Tools

Emma emphasized the role of visualization tools in presenting data insights. "Visualization tools transform data into visual representations," she noted. "They help us communicate insights effectively and make data more accessible to our teams."

David suggested using data visualization tools like D3.js or QlikView. "Data visualization tools provide customizable and interactive visualizations," he explained. "They enable us to create compelling charts, graphs, and maps that highlight key insights."

Lisa highlighted the importance of integrating visualization tools with our BI platforms. "Integrating visualization tools with our BI platforms ensures seamless data exploration," she remarked. "It allows us to create comprehensive dashboards that combine multiple data sources and perspectives."

Machine Learning Platforms

Emma focused on the potential of machine learning platforms for advanced analytics. "Machine learning platforms enable us to build predictive models and automate decision-making," she noted. "They provide tools and frameworks for developing and deploying machine learning algorithms."

David suggested using platforms like TensorFlow or Azure Machine Learning. "Machine learning platforms offer powerful tools for model development and deployment," he explained. "They enable us to leverage machine learning for tasks such as customer segmentation, demand forecasting, and anomaly detection."

Lisa emphasized the importance of collaboration between data scientists and domain experts. "Collaboration ensures that our machine learning models are relevant and accurate," she remarked. "We should foster cross-functional teams that combine data science expertise with business knowledge."

As the meeting concluded, the room was filled with a sense of excitement and anticipation. The leadership team at InnovateTech understood that selecting the right tools for data collection and analysis was crucial for their data-driven transformation. With a clear plan and a commitment to leveraging technology, they were ready to unlock the full potential of their data and drive their business forward.

Identifying Key Metrics

The air in the InnovateTech boardroom was charged with a sense of determination as the leadership team gathered once again. Today's focus was on identifying the key metrics that would guide their data-driven decision-making. Lisa, Emma, David, and their colleagues knew that selecting the right metrics was essential for measuring success and steering their company towards its goals.

Lisa, the CEO, opened the meeting with a confident tone. "To truly harness the power of our data, we need to identify the key metrics that matter most to our business," she began. "These metrics will serve as our navigational compass, helping us track performance, uncover insights, and make informed decisions."

David, ever the analytical thinker, nodded. "Metrics provide the quantitative foundation for our strategies," he said. "They allow us to objectively assess our progress, identify areas for improvement, and demonstrate the impact of our efforts."

Emma, the strategist, leaned forward. "Let's focus on defining a clear and comprehensive set of key metrics," she suggested. "We need metrics that align with our business objectives, resonate with our teams, and provide actionable insights."

Lisa clicked her remote, and the projector displayed a list of key areas where metrics could be applied. "We'll focus on six main categories: customer metrics, marketing metrics, sales metrics, financial metrics, operational metrics, and employee metrics," she explained. "Each category is crucial for a holistic view of our business performance."

Customer Metrics

Emma emphasized the importance of customer metrics in understanding and improving the customer experience. "Customer metrics help us gauge customer satisfaction, loyalty, and engagement," she noted. "They provide insights into how well we are meeting our customers' needs and expectations."

David suggested focusing on metrics such as Net Promoter Score (NPS) and Customer Satisfaction (CSAT) scores. "NPS measures the likelihood of customers recommending our products or services to others," he explained. "CSAT scores provide direct feedback on customer satisfaction with specific interactions or transactions."

Lisa highlighted the importance of Customer Lifetime Value (CLV). "CLV helps us understand the long-term value of our customers," she remarked. "It guides our strategies for customer retention, upselling, and cross-selling."

Marketing Metrics

Emma focused on the role of marketing metrics in assessing the effectiveness of their marketing campaigns. "Marketing metrics help us evaluate our marketing strategies, optimize our campaigns, and maximize our return on investment," she noted.

David suggested tracking metrics such as Cost Per Acquisition (CPA) and Return on Marketing Investment (ROMI). "CPA measures the cost of acquiring a new customer through our marketing efforts," he explained. "ROMI evaluates the profitability of our marketing investments."

Lisa emphasized the importance of Conversion Rates and Click-Through Rates (CTR). "Conversion rates indicate the percentage of visitors who take a desired action, such as making a purchase or signing up for a newsletter," she remarked. "CTR measures the effectiveness of our online ads and email campaigns."

Sales Metrics

Emma highlighted the significance of sales metrics in driving revenue growth. "Sales metrics provide insights into our sales performance, helping us identify strengths and areas for improvement," she noted.

David suggested focusing on metrics such as Sales Revenue and Sales Growth. "Sales revenue measures the total income generated from our sales activities," he explained. "Sales growth tracks the increase in revenue over a specific period, indicating our progress towards our growth targets."

Lisa emphasized the importance of metrics like Sales Conversion Rate and Average Deal Size. "The sales conversion rate measures the percentage of leads that convert into customers," she remarked. "Average deal size provides insights into the typical value of our sales transactions."

Financial Metrics

Emma stressed the need for financial metrics to ensure the financial health and sustainability of the business. "Financial metrics help us monitor our financial performance, manage costs, and drive profitability," she noted.

David suggested tracking metrics such as Gross Margin and Operating Margin. "Gross margin measures the difference between revenue and the cost of goods sold," he explained. "Operating margin indicates the percentage of revenue remaining after covering operating expenses."

Lisa highlighted the importance of metrics like Cash Flow and Return on Investment (ROI). "Cash flow measures the inflow and outflow of cash within the business," she remarked.

"ROI evaluates the profitability of our investments, helping us make informed investment decisions."

Operational Metrics

Emma focused on the role of operational metrics in improving efficiency and productivity. "Operational metrics help us assess the efficiency of our processes, identify bottlenecks, and drive continuous improvement," she noted.

David suggested tracking metrics such as Cycle Time and Throughput. "Cycle time measures the time taken to complete a specific process or task," he explained. "Throughput measures the rate at which we produce goods or services."

Lisa emphasized the importance of metrics like Inventory Turnover and Order Fulfillment Rate. "Inventory turnover measures how often we sell and replace our inventory," she remarked. "Order fulfillment rate indicates the percentage of orders delivered on time and in full."

Employee Metrics

Emma highlighted the significance of employee metrics in fostering a productive and engaged workforce. "Employee metrics help us understand and improve employee performance, satisfaction, and retention," she noted.

David suggested focusing on metrics such as Employee Engagement and Employee Retention Rate. "Employee engagement measures the level of commitment and enthusiasm employees have towards their work," he explained. "Employee retention rate tracks the percentage of employees who remain with the company over a specific period."

Lisa emphasized the importance of metrics like Training and Development Participation and Employee Productivity. "Training and development participation measures the involvement of employees in learning and growth opportunities," she remarked. "Employee productivity assesses the output and efficiency of our workforce."

As the meeting concluded, the room was filled with a sense of clarity and purpose. The leadership team at InnovateTech understood that identifying the right key metrics was essential for their data-driven transformation. With a comprehensive set of metrics in place, they were ready to navigate the complexities of their business with precision and insight, confident in their ability to achieve their goals and drive sustainable growth.

Analyzing Customer Behavior

The conference room at InnovateTech was abuzz with anticipation as the leadership team gathered to discuss one of the most crucial aspects of their data-driven strategy: analyzing customer behavior. Lisa, Emma, David, and their colleagues knew that understanding their customers' actions, preferences, and motivations was key to driving engagement, loyalty, and growth.

Lisa, the CEO, opened the meeting with a sense of excitement. "Today, we dive deep into the heart of our business—our customers," she began. "By analyzing customer behavior, we can tailor our offerings, enhance the customer experience, and ultimately drive loyalty and growth."

David, the analytical mind, nodded in agreement. "Customer behavior analysis provides insights into what our customers want, how they interact with our products, and what drives their purchasing decisions," he said. "It's about turning data into a powerful tool for customer-centric decision-making."

Emma, the strategist, leaned forward. "Let's explore the various dimensions of customer behavior and how we can leverage this understanding to create more value for our customers," she suggested. "We'll focus on six main aspects: customer journey mapping, purchase patterns, engagement metrics, sentiment analysis, churn prediction, and personalization."

Lisa clicked her remote, and the projector displayed a series of charts and graphs. "Let's start with customer journey mapping," she said.

Customer Journey Mapping

Emma highlighted the importance of mapping the customer journey. "Customer journey mapping involves tracking the steps a customer takes from initial awareness to post-purchase," she explained. "It helps us identify pain points, moments of delight, and opportunities to enhance the customer experience."

David suggested using tools like heat maps and funnel analysis to visualize customer interactions. "Heat maps show us where customers are clicking on our website, while funnel analysis helps us see where customers drop off in the buying process," he explained. "These tools provide valuable insights into how we can optimize our online experience."

Lisa emphasized the need for cross-functional collaboration in customer journey mapping. "Involving teams from marketing, sales, and customer service ensures we get a holistic view of the customer experience," she remarked. "It helps us identify and address issues at every touchpoint."

Purchase Patterns

Emma focused on analyzing purchase patterns to understand customer buying behavior. "By examining purchase patterns, we can identify trends, preferences, and seasonal variations in buying behavior," she noted. "This information helps us tailor our inventory, promotions, and marketing strategies."

David suggested using transaction data to analyze purchase frequency, average order value, and product combinations. "Transaction data provides a wealth of information about what, when, and how often customers buy," he explained. "It helps us identify our best-selling products, peak purchasing times, and complementary items."

Lisa highlighted the importance of segmenting customers based on purchase behavior. "Customer segmentation allows us to create targeted marketing campaigns for different customer groups," she remarked. "It helps us address the unique needs and preferences of each segment."

Engagement Metrics

Emma emphasized the role of engagement metrics in understanding customer interactions. "Engagement metrics track how customers interact with our brand across various channels," she noted. "They include website visits, social media interactions, email open rates, and more."

David suggested using analytics tools to monitor engagement metrics in real-time. "Real-time analytics provide up-to-date insights into customer behavior," he explained. "They help us identify which content and campaigns are resonating with our audience."

Lisa highlighted the importance of measuring customer engagement across the entire customer lifecycle. "Engagement metrics should cover all stages, from awareness to advocacy," she remarked. "It helps us understand how engaged customers are at each stage and identify opportunities to increase engagement."

Sentiment Analysis

Emma focused on the significance of sentiment analysis in gauging customer emotions. "Sentiment analysis uses natural language processing to analyze customer feedback and social media posts," she explained. "It helps us understand how customers feel about our brand and products."

David suggested leveraging sentiment analysis tools to monitor customer reviews and social media mentions. "These tools can analyze the tone and sentiment of customer feedback," he noted. "They provide insights into customer satisfaction, complaints, and areas for improvement."

Lisa emphasized the need to act on insights from sentiment analysis. "Understanding customer sentiment is only the first step," she remarked. "We need to take proactive steps to address negative feedback and enhance positive experiences."

Churn Prediction

Emma highlighted the importance of predicting customer churn to retain valuable customers. "Churn prediction models help us identify customers who are at risk of leaving," she noted. "They allow us to take preventive measures to retain these customers."

David suggested using machine learning algorithms to build churn prediction models. "Machine learning algorithms can analyze historical data to identify patterns that indicate churn risk," he explained. "They provide accurate predictions that help us target retention efforts effectively."

Lisa emphasized the need for personalized retention strategies. "Retention strategies should be tailored to the specific needs and preferences of at-risk customers," she remarked. "Personalized offers, targeted communications, and proactive customer service can make a significant difference."

Personalization

Emma focused on the power of personalization in enhancing the customer experience. "Personalization involves tailoring our interactions and offerings to individual customers based on their behavior and preferences," she explained. "It creates a more relevant and engaging experience for our customers."

David suggested using data to create personalized recommendations and offers. "Data-driven personalization can increase customer satisfaction and loyalty," he noted. "By analyzing customer behavior, we can recommend products, send targeted offers, and create personalized content."

Lisa highlighted the importance of respecting customer

privacy in personalization efforts. "While personalization enhances the customer experience, we must also prioritize customer privacy and data security," she remarked. "We should be transparent about how we use customer data and ensure that we comply with privacy regulations."

As the meeting concluded, the room was filled with a sense of clarity and purpose. The leadership team at InnovateTech understood that analyzing customer behavior was crucial for creating a customer-centric organization. With a deep understanding of their customers' actions, preferences, and motivations, they were ready to tailor their strategies to meet customer needs, enhance satisfaction, and drive long-term loyalty.

Predictive Analytics in Sales and Marketing

The InnovateTech boardroom was filled with anticipation as the leadership team gathered once more, this time to explore the transformative potential of predictive analytics in their sales and marketing efforts. Lisa, Emma, David, and their colleagues were eager to understand how leveraging advanced analytics could propel their company into a future of proactive, data-driven decisions.

Lisa, the CEO, opened the meeting with a forward-looking vision. "Predictive analytics is about harnessing data to foresee future trends and behaviors," she began. "It's not just about understanding where we are today but anticipating where we can go tomorrow."

David, the data guru, nodded. "Predictive analytics uses historical data, machine learning algorithms, and statistical techniques to predict future outcomes," he explained. "It's about transforming data into foresight, enabling us to make more informed, strategic decisions."

Emma, the strategist, leaned forward with excitement. "Let's dive into how predictive analytics can revolutionize both our sales and marketing strategies," she suggested. "We'll focus on six key areas: demand forecasting, lead scoring, customer lifetime value prediction, campaign optimization, churn prediction, and product recommendations."

Lisa clicked her remote, and the projector displayed an array of colorful graphs and predictive models. "We'll start with demand forecasting," she said.

Demand Forecasting

Emma highlighted the importance of demand forecasting in planning and resource allocation. "Demand forecasting allows us to predict future sales based on historical data and market trends," she explained. "It helps us optimize inventory, allocate resources, and plan production."

David suggested using time series analysis and machine learning models for accurate forecasts. "Time series analysis can identify patterns and trends in historical sales data," he explained. "Machine learning models, like ARIMA and LSTM, can provide even more precise predictions by accounting for various influencing factors."

Lisa emphasized the need for integrating demand forecasts into strategic planning. "Accurate demand forecasts enable us to align our production schedules, marketing campaigns, and sales efforts," she remarked. "It ensures we meet customer demand without overproducing or underproducing."

Lead Scoring

Emma focused on the role of predictive analytics in lead scoring. "Lead scoring uses predictive models to evaluate and prioritize leads based on their likelihood to convert," she noted. "It helps our sales team focus on the most promising prospects."

David suggested leveraging logistic regression and decision tree algorithms for lead scoring models. "These algorithms analyze various attributes and behaviors of leads to predict their conversion probability," he explained. "They help us identify high-quality leads and allocate our sales resources effectively."

Lisa highlighted the importance of continuously refining lead scoring models. "As we gather more data and insights, we can improve the accuracy of our lead scoring models," she remarked. "It's an ongoing process of learning and optimization."

Customer Lifetime Value Prediction

Emma emphasized the significance of predicting customer lifetime value (CLV). "CLV prediction estimates the total revenue a customer will generate over their relationship with our company," she explained. "It guides our customer acquisition and retention strategies."

David suggested using regression models and cohort analysis for CLV prediction. "Regression models can analyze historical purchase data to predict future spending patterns," he noted. "Cohort analysis helps us understand the behavior of different customer groups over time."

Lisa highlighted the strategic value of CLV prediction. "Knowing the potential lifetime value of our customers allows us to allocate marketing budgets more effectively and tailor retention efforts to high-value customers," she remarked.

Campaign Optimization

Emma focused on optimizing marketing campaigns using predictive analytics. "Predictive analytics can identify which campaign strategies are likely to yield the best results," she noted. "It helps us maximize the return on our marketing investments."

David suggested using A/B testing and multivariate analysis to optimize campaigns. "A/B testing compares different campaign variations to identify the most effective one," he explained. "Multivariate analysis examines multiple factors to determine the optimal combination of elements."

Lisa emphasized the importance of agility in campaign optimization. "Real-time data and predictive insights allow us to adapt our campaigns quickly," she remarked. "We can pivot strategies based on emerging trends and audience responses."

Churn Prediction

Emma highlighted the role of predictive analytics in identifying customers at risk of churning. "Churn prediction models help us foresee which customers are likely to leave," she explained. "It allows us to take proactive measures to retain them."

David suggested using survival analysis and random forest algorithms for churn prediction. "Survival analysis estimates the time until a customer churns based on their behavior," he noted. "Random forest algorithms can identify key factors contributing to churn."

Lisa emphasized the need for targeted retention strategies based on churn predictions. "Predictive insights enable us to design personalized retention campaigns for at-risk customers," she remarked. "It helps us reduce churn and enhance customer loyalty."

Product Recommendations

Emma focused on the power of predictive analytics in generating personalized product recommendations. "Predictive models analyze customer behavior and preferences to suggest relevant products," she explained. "It enhances the customer experience and drives cross-selling and upselling."

David suggested using collaborative filtering and matrix factorization techniques for product recommendations. "Collaborative filtering analyzes similarities between customers and items to make recommendations," he noted. "Matrix factorization decomposes the interaction matrix to uncover latent factors influencing preferences."

Lisa highlighted the importance of continuous learning in recommendation systems. "Our recommendation models should evolve with changing customer preferences and behavior," she remarked. "It ensures we provide timely and relevant suggestions."

As the meeting concluded, the room was filled with a sense of optimism and excitement. The leadership team at InnovateTech understood that predictive analytics was not just a tool, but a strategic asset that could transform their sales and marketing efforts. With a commitment to leveraging advanced analytics, they were ready to anticipate trends, optimize strategies, and drive future growth, confident in their ability to stay ahead of the curve in an ever-evolving market.

Using Data to Improve Strategies

The InnovateTech boardroom was filled with an air of determination as the leadership team gathered to discuss the final piece of their data-driven puzzle: using data to improve their strategies. Lisa, Emma, David, and their colleagues were eager to harness the power of data to refine their approach and drive innovation across the company.

Lisa, the CEO, began the meeting with a tone of resolve. "We've explored how to collect data, analyze it, and predict future trends," she said. "Now, it's time to talk about how we can use this data to continuously improve our strategies and stay ahead in the market."

David, the analytical expert, nodded. "Data is the foundation of our strategic decision-making," he agreed. "By analyzing past performance and current trends, we can refine our strategies, optimize our operations, and drive better outcomes."

Emma, the strategist, leaned forward with enthusiasm. "Let's focus on how we can use data to enhance our strategies across six key areas: market segmentation, product development, customer engagement, sales optimization, marketing effectiveness, and competitive analysis."

Lisa clicked her remote, and the projector displayed a series of charts and data visualizations. "We'll start with market segmentation," she said.

Market Segmentation

Emma highlighted the importance of using data for precise market segmentation. "Data allows us to segment our market based on various criteria such as demographics, behavior, and preferences," she explained. "It helps us target the right audience with tailored messages and offerings."

David suggested leveraging clustering algorithms and data mining techniques for segmentation. "Clustering algorithms like K-means can group customers into segments based on similarities in their behavior and characteristics," he explained. "Data mining helps us uncover hidden patterns and insights within these segments."

Lisa emphasized the strategic value of refined market segmentation. "Accurate segmentation enables us to create highly targeted marketing campaigns and product offerings," she remarked. "It increases our relevance to different customer groups and drives engagement and conversion."

Product Development

Emma focused on the role of data in guiding product development. "Data provides insights into customer needs, preferences, and pain points," she noted. "It helps us develop products that meet market demands and address gaps."

David suggested using sentiment analysis and feedback loops to inform product development. "Sentiment analysis can gauge customer reactions to existing products and identify areas for improvement," he explained. "Feedback loops involve continuously collecting and analyzing customer feedback to iterate on product designs."

Lisa highlighted the importance of data-driven innovation. "By incorporating data into our product development process, we can innovate more effectively and create products that resonate with our customers," she remarked. "It ensures we stay competitive and meet evolving market needs."

Customer Engagement

Emma emphasized the significance of using data to enhance customer engagement. "Data helps us understand how customers interact with our brand and what drives their engagement," she explained. "It allows us to create personalized experiences that foster loyalty and satisfaction."

David suggested leveraging customer journey analytics and engagement metrics. "Customer journey analytics track interactions across different touchpoints to identify key engagement drivers," he noted. "Engagement metrics measure the effectiveness of our engagement strategies and highlight areas for improvement."

Lisa highlighted the need for continuous optimization of engagement strategies. "Using data to refine our engagement strategies ensures we deliver consistent and meaningful experiences," she remarked. "It helps us build stronger relationships with our customers."

Sales Optimization

Emma focused on the role of data in optimizing sales strategies. "Data-driven insights can identify opportunities to improve our sales processes, increase efficiency, and drive revenue growth," she noted. "It helps us optimize lead management, sales pitches, and closing techniques."

David suggested using sales performance analytics and predictive models. "Sales performance analytics measure the effectiveness of different sales activities and identify areas for improvement," he explained. "Predictive models forecast sales trends and guide resource allocation."

Lisa emphasized the importance of data-driven sales management. "Optimizing our sales strategies based on data ensures we maximize our efforts and achieve our sales targets," she remarked. "It helps us stay agile and responsive to market changes."

Marketing Effectiveness

Emma highlighted the importance of using data to evaluate and improve marketing effectiveness. "Data provides insights into the performance of our marketing campaigns and channels," she explained. "It helps us allocate budgets effectively and optimize our marketing mix."

David suggested leveraging marketing analytics and ROI analysis. "Marketing analytics track key metrics such as reach, engagement, and conversion rates," he noted. "ROI analysis evaluates the profitability of our marketing investments and guides budget allocation."

Lisa emphasized the need for continuous measurement and adjustment. "Using data to measure marketing effectiveness allows us to make informed decisions and adjust our strategies in real-time," she remarked. "It ensures we achieve our marketing goals and drive business growth."

Competitive Analysis

Emma focused on the role of data in competitive analysis. "Data helps us monitor and analyze competitor activities, market trends, and industry dynamics," she explained. "It provides valuable insights into our competitive positioning and strategic opportunities."

David suggested using competitive intelligence tools and benchmarking techniques. "Competitive intelligence tools gather data on competitor strategies, pricing, and market share," he noted. "Benchmarking compares our performance against industry standards and best practices."

Lisa highlighted the strategic value of competitive analysis. "Using data for competitive analysis enables us to identify strengths, weaknesses, opportunities, and threats," she remarked. "It helps us develop strategies to outperform competitors and capture market share."

As the meeting concluded, the room was filled with a sense of purpose and clarity. The leadership team at InnovateTech understood that using data to continuously improve their strategies was crucial for staying competitive and driving growth. With a commitment to leveraging data-driven insights, they were ready to refine their approaches, optimize their operations, and achieve their strategic objectives, confident in their ability to navigate the complexities of an ever-evolving market.

9

Chapter 9: Content Marketing for Sales Enablement

Creating High-Impact Content

The atmosphere in the InnovateTech boardroom was electric as the team assembled to tackle a critical element of their strategy: creating high-impact content for sales enablement. Lisa, Emma, David, and their colleagues were well aware that compelling content could be a game-changer in driving engagement and conversions.

Lisa, the CEO, opened the meeting with a sense of urgency. "Today, we dive into the heart of our content marketing strategy," she began. "Creating high-impact content is not just about producing volume; it's about producing value. It's the key to empowering our sales team and engaging our audience."

David, the data guru, chimed in. "High-impact content is informed by data and tailored to meet the specific needs and pain points of our target audience," he explained. "It's about creating content that resonates and drives action."

Emma, the strategist, leaned forward with enthusiasm. "Let's focus on how we can create content that not only captivates our audience but also empowers our sales team," she suggested. "We'll look at six critical steps: understanding your audience, setting clear objectives, crafting compelling messages, using the right formats, leveraging storytelling, and ensuring consistency."

Lisa clicked her remote, and the projector displayed an array of content strategies and examples. "We'll start with understanding your audience," she said.

Understanding Your Audience

Emma highlighted the importance of audience insights. "To create high-impact content, we must first understand our audience deeply," she explained. "This involves researching their demographics, behaviors, preferences, and pain points."

David suggested using data analytics and customer surveys to gather insights. "Data analytics can reveal trends and patterns in customer behavior," he noted. "Customer surveys and feedback provide qualitative insights into their needs and challenges."

Lisa emphasized the need for detailed buyer personas. "Creating detailed buyer personas helps us tailor our content to specific segments of our audience," she remarked. "It ensures our messages are relevant and impactful."

Setting Clear Objectives

Emma focused on the role of clear objectives in content creation. "Every piece of content should serve a specific purpose," she noted. "Whether it's to educate, entertain, or persuade, setting clear objectives ensures our content drives the desired action."

David suggested using SMART criteria for setting objectives. "Objectives should be Specific, Measurable, Achievable, Relevant, and Time-bound," he explained. "This framework helps us stay focused and measure our success."

Lisa highlighted the importance of aligning content objectives with business goals. "Our content objectives should align with our overall business goals," she remarked. "It ensures our content contributes to our strategic priorities and delivers measurable results."

Crafting Compelling Messages

Emma emphasized the significance of compelling messages in high-impact content. "Our messages should be clear, concise, and compelling," she explained. "They should address our audience's pain points and highlight the value we offer."

David suggested using storytelling techniques to enhance messages. "Storytelling makes our messages more engaging and memorable," he noted. "By framing our value propositions within relatable stories, we can connect with our audience on an emotional level."

Lisa highlighted the need for authenticity in messaging. "Authentic messages resonate more with our audience," she remarked. "We should be genuine and transparent in our communication, building trust and credibility."

Using the Right Formats

Emma focused on the importance of choosing the right content formats. "Different formats appeal to different audience segments and stages of the buyer journey," she noted. "We should use a mix of formats, including blogs, videos, infographics, and case studies."

David suggested leveraging data to identify the most effective formats. "Data can reveal which formats our audience prefers and engages with most," he explained. "It helps us allocate our resources to the formats that deliver the best results."

Lisa emphasized the need for versatility in content creation. "We should be versatile in our content creation, experimenting with new formats and adapting to changing preferences," she remarked. "It ensures we stay relevant and engaging."

Leveraging Storytelling

Emma highlighted the power of storytelling in content marketing. "Storytelling transforms facts and figures into compelling narratives," she explained. "It makes our content more relatable and impactful."

David suggested using customer stories and testimonials to enhance storytelling. "Customer stories and testimonials add authenticity to our narratives," he noted. "They showcase real-life examples of how our solutions have made a difference."

Lisa emphasized the importance of a consistent brand story. "Our brand story should be consistent across all content," she remarked. "It creates a cohesive narrative that reinforces our brand identity and values."

Ensuring Consistency

Emma focused on the need for consistency in content marketing. "Consistency in tone, style, and messaging is crucial for building brand recognition and trust," she noted. "It ensures our content feels cohesive and professional."

David suggested creating a content style guide to ensure consistency. "A content style guide outlines the standards for tone, style, and formatting," he explained. "It ensures all content aligns with our brand guidelines."

Lisa highlighted the importance of regular content audits. "Regular content audits help us ensure our content remains relevant and aligned with our objectives," she remarked. "It allows us to identify gaps and opportunities for improvement."

As the meeting concluded, the room was filled with a sense of clarity and determination. The leadership team at InnovateTech understood that creating high-impact content was essential for empowering their sales team and engaging their audience. With a commitment to understanding their audience, setting clear objectives, crafting compelling messages, using the right formats, leveraging storytelling, and ensuring consistency, they were ready to elevate their content marketing strategy and drive impactful results.

Content Personalization

The InnovateTech boardroom was buzzing with excitement as the leadership team reconvened to tackle the next crucial element of their strategy: content personalization. Lisa, Emma, David, and their colleagues understood that in today's market, one-size-fits-all content wouldn't cut it. Personalization was key to resonating with their diverse audience and driving engagement.

Lisa, the CEO, started the meeting with a confident tone. "Personalization is the cornerstone of effective content marketing," she began. "It's about delivering the right message to the right person at the right time. When done correctly, personalized content can significantly boost our engagement and conversion rates."

David, the data guru, nodded in agreement. "Personalization relies on data to understand individual preferences and behaviors," he explained. "By leveraging customer data, we can tailor our content to meet the specific needs and interests of each audience segment."

Emma, the strategist, leaned forward with enthusiasm. "Let's explore how we can implement content personalization effectively," she suggested. "We'll focus on six key strategies: collecting and analyzing customer data, segmenting your audience, creating dynamic content, leveraging AI and machine learning, implementing personalization across channels, and measuring the impact."

Lisa clicked her remote, and the projector displayed a roadmap for content personalization. "We'll start with collecting and analyzing customer data," she said.

Collecting and Analyzing Customer Data

Emma emphasized the importance of robust data collection and analysis. "To personalize content, we need to gather comprehensive data about our customers," she explained. "This includes demographics, behavior, purchase history, and interactions with our brand."

David suggested using various data collection methods, including web analytics, CRM systems, and social media insights. "Web analytics tools can track user behavior on our website," he noted. "CRM systems store valuable customer information, and social media platforms provide insights into customer preferences and interactions."

Lisa highlighted the need for data privacy and security. "As we collect and analyze customer data, we must ensure we comply with data privacy regulations and protect our customers' information," she remarked. "Trust is paramount in building lasting relationships."

Segmenting Your Audience

Emma focused on the role of audience segmentation in personalization. "Segmentation allows us to group customers based on shared characteristics and behaviors," she noted. "It helps us create targeted content that addresses the specific needs and interests of each segment."

David suggested using clustering algorithms and machine learning models for effective segmentation. "Clustering algorithms can identify natural groupings within our customer base," he explained. "Machine learning models can further refine these segments based on evolving behaviors and preferences."

Lisa emphasized the strategic value of detailed segmentation. "By understanding the nuances within our audience, we can tailor our messages to be more relevant and impactful," she remarked. "It ensures we deliver personalized experiences at scale."

Creating Dynamic Content

Emma highlighted the significance of dynamic content in personalization. "Dynamic content changes based on user data and interactions," she explained. "It allows us to deliver personalized messages in real-time, enhancing the user experience."

David suggested using content management systems (CMS) with dynamic content capabilities. "A CMS with dynamic content features can display different content variations based on user attributes and behaviors," he noted. "It ensures each visitor sees content that is most relevant to them."

Lisa emphasized the importance of testing and optimization. "We should continuously test and optimize our dynamic content to ensure it delivers the desired results," she remarked. "A/B testing and multivariate testing can help us identify the most effective content variations."

Leveraging AI and Machine Learning

Emma focused on the role of AI and machine learning in content personalization. "AI and machine learning algorithms can analyze vast amounts of data and identify patterns," she noted. "They can predict customer preferences and deliver personalized content at scale."

David suggested using recommendation engines and predictive analytics. "Recommendation engines analyze user behavior to suggest relevant content and products," he explained. "Predictive analytics can forecast future behaviors and preferences, allowing us to proactively tailor our content."

Lisa highlighted the need for continuous learning and adaptation. "AI and machine learning models should continuously learn and adapt based on new data," she remarked. "It ensures our personalization efforts remain effective and up-to-date."

Implementing Personalization Across Channels

Emma emphasized the importance of a multi-channel personalization strategy. "Customers interact with our brand across various channels, including our website, email, social media, and mobile apps," she explained. "We need to deliver personalized experiences consistently across all these touchpoints."

David suggested using omnichannel marketing platforms. "Omnichannel marketing platforms integrate data and interactions across different channels," he noted. "They enable us to deliver a seamless and personalized customer journey."

Lisa highlighted the strategic value of channel integration. "Integrating our personalization efforts across channels ensures we provide a cohesive and engaging experience," she remarked. "It enhances customer satisfaction and loyalty."

CHAPTER 9: CONTENT MARKETING FOR SALES ENABLEMENT

Measuring the Impact

Emma focused on the importance of measuring the impact of personalization efforts. "To evaluate the effectiveness of our personalization strategy, we need to track key metrics and analyze the results," she noted. "It helps us identify what works and where we can improve."

David suggested using metrics such as engagement rates, conversion rates, and customer satisfaction scores. "Engagement rates measure how well our personalized content resonates with our audience," he explained. "Conversion rates indicate the effectiveness of our personalized messages in driving actions, and customer satisfaction scores reflect overall customer experience."

Lisa emphasized the need for continuous improvement. "Personalization is an ongoing process," she remarked. "By continuously measuring and optimizing our efforts, we can ensure our content remains relevant and impactful."

As the meeting concluded, the room was filled with a sense of excitement and anticipation. The leadership team at InnovateTech understood that content personalization was essential for creating high-impact content that resonates with their audience. With a commitment to collecting and analyzing data, segmenting their audience, creating dynamic content, leveraging AI and machine learning, implementing personalization across channels, and measuring the impact, they were ready to elevate their content marketing strategy and drive meaningful engagement and conversions.

Aligning Content with Buyer's Journey

The InnovateTech boardroom was filled with focused energy as the leadership team gathered for the next session on content marketing: aligning content with the buyer's journey. Lisa, Emma, David, and their colleagues knew that delivering the right content at each stage of the buyer's journey was crucial for guiding prospects towards a purchase.

Lisa, the CEO, set the tone for the meeting with a sense of purpose. "Today, we focus on ensuring that our content meets our customers where they are in their journey," she began. "By aligning our content with the stages of the buyer's journey, we can nurture leads more effectively and drive them towards conversion."

David, the data guru, nodded. "Understanding the buyer's journey helps us deliver relevant content that addresses specific needs and questions at each stage," he explained. "It's about providing the right information at the right time."

Emma, the strategist, leaned forward with enthusiasm. "Let's break down the buyer's journey into three main stages: awareness, consideration, and decision," she suggested. "For each stage, we'll discuss the type of content that resonates most and how we can deliver it effectively."

Lisa clicked her remote, and the projector displayed a visual representation of the buyer's journey. "We'll start with the awareness stage," she said.

Awareness Stage

Emma highlighted the significance of the awareness stage. "At this stage, potential customers are just realizing they have a problem or need," she explained. "Our goal is to attract their attention and provide valuable information that helps them understand their challenges."

David suggested using educational content such as blog posts, eBooks, and infographics. "Educational content helps prospects learn more about their problems and possible solutions," he noted. "It positions us as a knowledgeable and trustworthy resource."

Lisa emphasized the importance of SEO and social media in the awareness stage. "SEO ensures our content is easily discoverable when prospects search for information," she remarked. "Social media helps us reach a broader audience and engage with them effectively."

Consideration Stage

Emma focused on the role of content in the consideration stage. "In this stage, prospects are evaluating different solutions to their problems," she noted. "Our content should help them compare options and understand how our solutions stand out."

David suggested using case studies, comparison guides, and webinars. "Case studies provide real-life examples of how our solutions have helped others," he explained. "Comparison guides highlight our competitive advantages, and webinars offer in-depth insights and interactive engagement."

Lisa highlighted the need for targeted nurturing campaigns.

"We should use email nurturing campaigns to deliver relevant content to prospects based on their interactions and interests," she remarked. "It helps us stay top of mind and build deeper relationships."

Decision Stage

Emma emphasized the importance of content in the decision stage. "At this stage, prospects are ready to make a purchase decision," she explained. "Our content should address any remaining concerns and provide the final push towards conversion."

David suggested using product demos, testimonials, and free trials. "Product demos showcase our solutions in action, building confidence in our offerings," he noted. "Testimonials from satisfied customers provide social proof, and free trials allow prospects to experience our solutions firsthand."

Lisa highlighted the need for personalized follow-ups. "Personalized follow-ups from our sales team can address specific questions and concerns," she remarked. "It ensures prospects feel valued and supported in their decision-making process."

Creating a Seamless Journey

Emma focused on the importance of creating a seamless buyer's journey. "Our content should flow naturally from one stage to the next, guiding prospects smoothly through their journey," she noted. "Consistency in messaging and branding is key to building trust and continuity."

David suggested using marketing automation tools to

streamline content delivery. "Marketing automation tools can segment our audience and deliver personalized content based on their stage in the journey," he explained. "It ensures timely and relevant interactions."

Lisa emphasized the strategic value of a cohesive content strategy. "A cohesive content strategy ensures all our efforts are aligned towards guiding prospects through the buyer's journey," she remarked. "It maximizes our chances of converting leads into loyal customers."

Measuring Effectiveness

Emma highlighted the importance of measuring the effectiveness of content at each stage. "To refine our strategy, we need to track key metrics such as engagement rates, lead progression, and conversion rates," she explained. "It helps us identify what works and where we can improve."

David suggested using analytics tools to monitor content performance. "Analytics tools provide insights into how prospects interact with our content at each stage," he noted. "It allows us to make data-driven adjustments and optimize our approach."

Lisa emphasized the need for continuous improvement. "The buyer's journey is dynamic, and our content strategy should evolve with it," she remarked. "By continuously measuring and refining our efforts, we can ensure our content remains relevant and impactful."

As the meeting concluded, the room was filled with a sense of clarity and determination. The leadership team at InnovateTech understood that aligning their content with the buyer's journey was essential for nurturing leads and driving conversions. With a commitment to delivering the right content at each stage, creating a seamless journey, and measuring effectiveness, they were ready to elevate their content marketing strategy and guide prospects towards making informed purchase decisions.

Utilizing Different Content Formats

The InnovateTech boardroom was alive with anticipation as the team reconvened to explore the next crucial aspect of their content marketing strategy: utilizing different content formats. Lisa, Emma, David, and their colleagues recognized that a diverse array of content formats could cater to various audience preferences and consumption habits, enhancing engagement and reach.

Lisa, the CEO, opened the meeting with an enthusiastic tone. "Today, we delve into the power of diverse content formats," she began. "Using a variety of formats allows us to reach different segments of our audience more effectively and keep our content fresh and engaging."

David, the data guru, agreed. "Different formats can appeal to different learning styles and preferences," he explained. "By offering a mix of content types, we can ensure we meet our audience where they are and how they prefer to consume information."

Emma, the strategist, leaned forward with a plan. "Let's break down the various content formats we can utilize," she suggested. "We'll focus on six key formats: blog posts, videos, infographics, podcasts, webinars, and interactive content. Each format has its unique strengths and can play a critical role in our overall strategy."

Lisa clicked her remote, and the projector displayed an array of content formats. "We'll start with blog posts," she said.

Blog Posts

Emma highlighted the enduring value of blog posts. "Blog posts are foundational to our content strategy," she explained. "They provide in-depth information, enhance our SEO, and establish us as thought leaders in our industry."

David suggested using a mix of how-to guides, industry news, and opinion pieces. "How-to guides offer practical advice, industry news keeps our audience informed, and opinion pieces showcase our expertise and perspective," he noted. "A variety of blog post types keeps our content engaging and relevant."

Lisa emphasized the importance of consistency and quality. "Regular, high-quality blog posts build trust and keep our audience coming back for more," she remarked. "We should maintain a consistent publishing schedule and ensure each post delivers value."

Videos

Emma focused on the growing popularity of video content. "Videos are highly engaging and can convey complex information quickly and effectively," she noted. "They are perfect for product demos, customer testimonials, and behind-the-scenes looks at our company."

David suggested leveraging platforms like YouTube and social media for video distribution. "Publishing videos on platforms like YouTube expands our reach and enhances our

SEO," he explained. "Social media platforms like Facebook and Instagram allow us to engage with our audience through live streams and short-form videos."

Lisa highlighted the importance of storytelling in videos. "Videos should tell compelling stories that resonate with our audience," she remarked. "Whether it's showcasing customer success stories or providing a glimpse into our company culture, storytelling makes our videos memorable."

Infographics

Emma emphasized the visual appeal of infographics. "Infographics are excellent for presenting data and statistics in a visually engaging way," she explained. "They can simplify complex information and make it more accessible to our audience."

David suggested using infographics to complement blog posts and reports. "Infographics can be embedded in blog posts or included in reports to enhance understanding," he noted. "They are also highly shareable on social media, increasing our content's reach."

Lisa highlighted the need for clarity and design. "Infographics should be clear, visually appealing, and easy to understand," she remarked. "Good design ensures our key messages are effectively communicated."

Podcasts

Emma focused on the rise of podcasts as a content format. "Podcasts are growing in popularity and offer a convenient way for our audience to consume content on the go," she noted.

"They are perfect for in-depth discussions, interviews, and industry insights."

David suggested creating a series of podcast episodes on relevant topics. "A podcast series allows us to delve deep into various subjects and build a loyal audience over time," he explained. "We can feature industry experts, discuss trends, and share our company's journey."

Lisa emphasized the importance of quality production. "High-quality audio and engaging content are crucial for a successful podcast," she remarked. "Professional production ensures our podcasts are enjoyable and easy to listen to."

Webinars

Emma highlighted the interactive nature of webinars. "Webinars provide a platform for live interaction with our audience," she explained. "They are ideal for product demonstrations, training sessions, and expert panels."

David suggested using webinars to generate leads and nurture relationships. "Webinars can capture valuable leads and provide opportunities for real-time engagement," he noted. "Follow-up emails and surveys can help nurture these leads and gather feedback."

Lisa emphasized the importance of preparation and engagement. "Well-prepared webinars with interactive elements like Q&A sessions and polls keep our audience engaged," she remarked. "Preparation ensures we deliver valuable and impactful sessions."

Interactive Content

Emma focused on the growing trend of interactive content. "Interactive content, such as quizzes, calculators, and interactive infographics, engages our audience in a dynamic way," she noted. "It encourages participation and enhances user experience."

David suggested using interactive content to personalize the user journey. "Interactive content can provide personalized recommendations and insights based on user inputs," he explained. "It creates a more tailored and engaging experience."

Lisa emphasized the strategic use of interactivity. "Strategic use of interactive content can drive deeper engagement and capture valuable data," she remarked. "It enhances our understanding of

our audience and allows us to tailor future content more effectively."

Creating a Comprehensive Content Mix

Lisa clicked her remote, and the projector illuminated the room with a comprehensive overview of the content mix. "We'll start with blog posts," she announced.

Blog Posts

Emma emphasized the importance of blog posts in driving organic traffic and establishing thought leadership. "Blog posts are foundational to our content strategy," she explained. "They help us address common questions, share industry insights, and provide valuable information that attracts and engages our audience. By consistently publishing high-quality blog posts, we can improve our search engine rankings and drive more traffic to our website."

David suggested incorporating videos to enhance engagement and convey complex information in an easily digestible format. "Videos are incredibly powerful in capturing attention and conveying messages quickly," he noted. "They allow us to showcase product demonstrations, share customer testimonials, and provide educational content in a visually engaging way. Videos can be shared across multiple platforms, increasing our reach and impact."

Infographics

Lisa highlighted the effectiveness of infographics in simplifying complex information and making it visually appealing. "Infographics are excellent for presenting data and statistics in a way that's easy to understand and share," she remarked. "They can help us communicate key messages quickly and effectively, making them a valuable addition to our content mix."

eBooks

Emma suggested creating eBooks to provide in-depth information and establish authority on specific topics. "eBooks allow us to delve deeper into subjects and provide comprehensive insights to our audience," she explained. "They can be used as lead magnets to capture contact information and nurture potential customers through the sales funnel."

David proposed incorporating podcasts to reach audiences

who prefer audio content. "Podcasts are growing in popularity and offer a convenient way for people to consume content on the go," he noted. "We can use podcasts to share interviews with industry experts, discuss trends, and provide valuable insights that our audience can listen to during their commute or while multitasking."

Webinars

Lisa concluded with the importance of webinars in engaging prospects and providing interactive learning experiences. "Webinars allow us to connect with our audience in real-time, answer their questions, and provide valuable information in an engaging format," she said. "They can help us build relationships, generate leads, and move prospects further down the sales funnel."

As the discussion continued, the team explored the intricacies of creating a comprehensive content mix, recognizing its importance in engaging their audience and driving sales. With a strategic approach to utilizing different content formats, they were poised to capture attention, spark interest, and drive action, ultimately achieving their content marketing and sales enablement goals.

Measuring Content Effectiveness

The atmosphere in the InnovateTech boardroom was charged with anticipation as the team continued their discussion, now focusing on the critical aspect of measuring content effectiveness. Lisa, Emma, David, and their colleagues understood that without proper measurement, their content marketing efforts

CHAPTER 9: CONTENT MARKETING FOR SALES ENABLEMENT

would lack direction and fail to deliver the desired results.

Lisa, the CEO, set the tone for the discussion with a determined tone. "Today, we dive into the realm of metrics and analytics," she began. "Measuring the effectiveness of our content is essential for refining our strategy, optimizing our efforts, and driving meaningful results."

David, the data guru, nodded in agreement. "Data is the backbone of effective content marketing," he explained. "By analyzing key metrics, we can gain insights into how our content performs, what resonates with our audience, and where we can improve."

Emma, the strategist, leaned forward with a plan. "Let's explore the various metrics we should track to measure content effectiveness," she suggested. "We'll focus on six key areas: engagement metrics, conversion metrics, audience metrics, SEO metrics, social media metrics, and content performance metrics."

Lisa clicked her remote, and the projector displayed a comprehensive dashboard of metrics and analytics. "We'll start with engagement metrics," she said.

Engagement Metrics

Emma highlighted the importance of engagement metrics in evaluating content performance. "Engagement metrics measure how actively our audience interacts with our content," she explained. "They include metrics such as page views, time on page, bounce rate, and social shares."

David suggested using engagement metrics to assess content resonance. "High engagement indicates that our content resonates with our audience and captures their attention," he noted. "Low engagement may indicate that our content needs improvement or better targeting."

Lisa emphasized the need for context in interpreting engagement metrics. "Engagement metrics should be analyzed in the context of our goals and objectives," she remarked. "A high bounce rate may not always be negative if visitors are finding the information they need quickly."

Conversion Metrics

Emma focused on the significance of conversion metrics in measuring content effectiveness. "Conversion metrics track how well our content drives desired actions, such as signups, downloads, and purchases," she noted. "They include metrics such as conversion rate, click-through rate, and lead generation."

David suggested using conversion metrics to assess content relevance and effectiveness. "High conversion rates indicate that our content effectively persuades and motivates our audience to take action," he explained. "Low conversion rates may indicate that our content needs optimization or better alignment with audience needs."

Lisa highlighted the importance of tracking conversions throughout the customer journey. "Understanding how content contributes to conversions at each stage of the buyer's journey helps us optimize our content strategy," she remarked. "It ensures our content is driving meaningful results."

Audience Metrics

Emma emphasized the value of audience metrics in understanding content reach and impact. "Audience metrics provide insights into who our content is reaching and how they are engaging with it," she explained. "They include metrics such as demographics, geographic location, and device usage."

David suggested using audience metrics to tailor content to audience preferences. "Understanding our audience demographics and preferences helps us create content that resonates with their interests and needs," he noted. "It ensures our content remains relevant and impactful."

Lisa highlighted the importance of audience segmentation in content strategy. "Segmenting our audience allows us to deliver personalized content that speaks directly to their unique needs and interests," she remarked. "It enhances engagement and builds stronger relationships with our audience."

SEO Metrics

Emma focused on the role of SEO metrics in content visibility and discoverability. "SEO metrics track how well our content performs in search engine results pages," she explained. "They include metrics such as organic traffic, keyword rankings, and backlink profile."

David suggested using SEO metrics to optimize content for search intent. "Understanding search intent helps us create content that aligns with what our audience is searching for," he noted. "It improves our content's visibility and drives organic traffic."

Lisa emphasized the need for ongoing SEO optimization.

"SEO is an ongoing process that requires regular monitoring and adjustment," she remarked. "By continuously optimizing our content for SEO, we can improve its visibility and reach."

Social Media Metrics

Emma highlighted the importance of social media metrics in assessing content engagement and virality. "Social media metrics track how well our content performs on social media platforms," she explained. "They include metrics such as likes, shares, comments, and follower growth."

David suggested using social media metrics to identify content trends and preferences. "Analyzing social media metrics helps us understand which types of content resonate most with our audience," he noted. "It informs our content strategy and helps us create more engaging content."

Lisa emphasized the need for active engagement on social media platforms. "Social media is a two-way conversation," she remarked. "Engaging with our audience through comments, messages, and shares helps build relationships and foster loyalty."

Content Performance Metrics

Emma focused on the role of content performance metrics in evaluating overall content effectiveness. "Content performance metrics provide insights into how well our content contributes to our business goals," she explained. "They include metrics such as ROI, cost per acquisition, and customer lifetime value."

David suggested using content performance metrics to

measure the impact of content on the bottom line. "Ultimately, content should drive meaningful business results," he noted. "Analyzing content performance metrics helps us assess the return on investment and make data-driven decisions."

Lisa highlighted the importance of aligning content performance metrics with business objectives. "Our content strategy should be aligned with our broader business goals," she remarked. "Measuring content performance against these goals ensures our content is delivering value and driving growth."

As the meeting concluded, the room was filled with a sense of purpose and determination. The leadership team at InnovateTech understood that measuring content effectiveness was essential for optimizing their content strategy and driving meaningful results. With a commitment to tracking engagement metrics, conversion metrics, audience metrics, SEO metrics, social media metrics, and content performance metrics, they were ready to elevate their content marketing efforts and achieve their business objectives.

Content Distribution Strategies

The InnovateTech boardroom hummed with energy as the team delved into the crucial topic of content distribution strategies. Lisa, Emma, David, and their colleagues understood that creating great content was only half the battle; getting it in front of the right audience was equally important for driving engagement and conversions.

Lisa, the CEO, opened the discussion with a determined expression. "Today, we explore the various avenues for distributing our content," she began. "Effective distribution strategies ensure that our content reaches our target audience and drives the desired actions."

David, the data guru, nodded in agreement. "Content distribution is all about maximizing the reach and impact of our content," he explained. "By leveraging the right channels and tactics, we can ensure our content gets the visibility it deserves."

Emma, the strategist, leaned forward with a plan. "Let's break down our content distribution strategies into six key areas: owned media, earned media, paid media, social media, email marketing, and influencer partnerships," she suggested. "Each channel offers unique opportunities to amplify our content and engage our audience."

Lisa clicked her remote, and the projector displayed a comprehensive overview of content distribution strategies. "We'll start with owned media," she said.

Owned Media

Emma highlighted the value of owned media in content distribution. "Owned media refers to channels that we control, such as our website, blog, and email list," she explained. "It allows us to have full control over our content and how it is presented to our audience."

David suggested optimizing owned media channels for content visibility. "We should ensure our website is user-friendly and optimized for search engines," he noted. "A well-designed blog with relevant and valuable content can attract and retain visitors."

Lisa emphasized the importance of consistency in owned media channels. "Regularly updating our blog and website with fresh content keeps our audience engaged and coming back for more," she remarked. "It establishes us as a reliable and authoritative source in our industry."

Earned Media

Emma focused on the power of earned media in content distribution. "Earned media refers to publicity gained through word-of-mouth, PR efforts, and media coverage," she explained. "It involves getting others to share and talk about our content organically."

David suggested leveraging media relationships and influencer outreach. "Building relationships with journalists and industry influencers can help us secure media coverage and endorsements," he noted. "Their endorsement adds credibility and amplifies our content's reach."

Lisa highlighted the importance of creating share-worthy content. "Content that is valuable, unique, and emotionally resonant is more likely to be shared by our audience," she remarked. "We should focus on creating content that adds value and sparks conversation."

Paid Media

Emma emphasized the role of paid media in content distribution. "Paid media involves paying for exposure through advertising channels such as PPC ads, sponsored content, and social media ads," she explained. "It allows us to reach a targeted audience and drive traffic to our content."

David suggested allocating budget strategically across paid media channels. "We should identify channels that align with our target audience and business objectives," he noted. "A mix of search, display, and social media ads can maximize our content's visibility and impact."

Lisa highlighted the importance of testing and optimization in paid media campaigns. "A/B testing different ad creatives, targeting options, and messaging helps us identify what resonates best with our audience," she remarked. "Continuous optimization ensures we get the most out of our ad spend."

Social Media

Emma turned to the power of social media in content distribution. "Social media platforms offer a powerful channel for distributing content and engaging with our audience," she noted. "Platforms like Facebook, Twitter, LinkedIn, and Instagram allow us to share our content with a wide audience and foster community engagement."

David suggested tailoring content for each social media platform. "Each social media platform has its own unique audience and content format preferences," he explained. "We should optimize our content for each platform to maximize engagement and reach."

Lisa emphasized the importance of engagement on social media. "Engaging with our audience through likes, comments, and shares helps us build relationships and foster loyalty," she remarked. "A strong social media presence boosts our brand's visibility and credibility."

Email Marketing

Emma highlighted the effectiveness of email marketing in content distribution. "Email marketing allows us to deliver personalized content directly to our audience's inbox," she explained. "It's perfect for nurturing leads, promoting new content, and driving conversions."

David suggested segmenting email lists for targeted content delivery. "Segmenting our email list based on demographics, interests, and behaviors allows us to send relevant content to each audience segment," he noted. "Personalization enhances engagement and drives results."

Lisa emphasized the importance of providing value in email content. "Email content should provide value to the recipient, whether it's educational information, exclusive offers, or updates on industry trends," she remarked. "Delivering value builds trust and keeps subscribers engaged."

Influencer Partnerships

Emma turned to the potential of influencer partnerships in content distribution. "Influencers have established credibility and large followings in specific niches," she explained. "Partnering with influencers allows us to tap into their audience and leverage their influence to amplify our content."

David suggested identifying influencers whose audience aligns with our target market. "We should research influencers who have a genuine connection with our industry and audience," he noted. "Authentic partnerships result in more impactful content distribution."

Lisa highlighted the importance of building relationships

with influencers. "Building genuine relationships with influencers based on mutual trust and respect lays the foundation for successful partnerships," she remarked. "Collaborating on content creation ensures alignment with our brand values and messaging."

Executing a Comprehensive Strategy

Emma leaned forward, summarizing the team's insights. "By leveraging a mix of owned media, earned media, paid media, social media, email marketing, and influencer partnerships, we can maximize the reach and impact of our content," she noted. "Each channel offers unique opportunities to engage our audience and drive meaningful results."

David nodded in agreement. "A comprehensive content distribution strategy ensures that our content gets the visibility it deserves and reaches our target audience effectively," he remarked. "Continuous monitoring and optimization help us adapt to changing trends and maximize our content's impact."

Lisa emphasized the need for experimentation and innovation. "Content distribution is an evolving landscape," she remarked. "By staying agile and open to new opportunities, we can continually refine our strategy and drive success."

As the meeting concluded, the room was filled with a sense of excitement and determination. The leadership team at InnovateTech understood that effective content distribution was essential for maximizing the impact of their content marketing efforts. With a commitment to leveraging diverse distribution channels and continuously optimizing their strategy, they were ready to elevate their content distribution game and achieve their business objectives.

10

Chapter 10: Digital Marketing Strategies

SEO Best Practices

In the bustling conference room of InnovateTech, the team gathered to delve into the intricate world of digital marketing strategies. Lisa, Emma, David, and their colleagues understood the pivotal role of SEO in driving online visibility and attracting organic traffic to their website.

Lisa, the CEO, set the stage with a determined tone. "Today, we unravel the mysteries of SEO and its importance in our digital marketing efforts," she declared. "SEO best practices are the foundation of our online presence, ensuring that our content ranks well in search engine results and reaches our target audience."

David, the data guru, nodded in agreement. "SEO is a dynamic field that requires continuous adaptation to ever-changing algorithms and user behaviors," he explained. "By implementing SEO best practices, we can improve our website's visibility, increase organic traffic, and ultimately drive conversions."

Emma, the strategist, leaned forward with a plan. "Let's explore the key SEO best practices that will elevate our digital marketing strategy," she suggested. "We'll focus on six critical areas: keyword research, on-page optimization, technical SEO, content quality, user experience, and link building."

Lisa clicked her remote, and the projector displayed a comprehensive overview of SEO best practices. "We'll start with keyword research," she said.

Keyword Research

Emma emphasized the importance of keyword research in SEO strategy. "Keyword research helps us understand what our target audience is searching for and tailor our content accordingly," she explained. "By identifying relevant keywords with high search volume and low competition, we can optimize our content for better visibility in search engine results."

David suggested using keyword research tools to identify valuable keywords. "Tools like Google Keyword Planner, SEMrush, and Moz Keyword Explorer provide valuable insights into keyword volume, competition, and related terms," he noted. "They help us identify opportunities to target keywords that align with our business objectives."

Lisa highlighted the need for a strategic approach to keyword targeting. "We should focus on long-tail keywords that are specific to our niche and have high intent," she remarked. "Targeting the right keywords ensures our content is relevant to our target audience and ranks well in search engine results."

On-Page Optimization

Emma turned to the importance of on-page optimization in SEO strategy. "On-page optimization involves optimizing individual web pages to rank higher and earn more relevant traffic in search engines," she explained. "It includes elements such as meta tags, headings, URL structure, and internal linking."

David suggested optimizing meta tags for improved click-through rates. "Meta tags, including meta titles and meta descriptions, are displayed in search engine results and influence user behavior," he noted. "Crafting compelling meta tags that accurately describe the content can increase click-through rates and drive more organic traffic."

Lisa emphasized the importance of creating high-quality, relevant content. "Content is the foundation of on-page optimization," she remarked. "We should focus on creating valuable, informative content that addresses the needs and interests of our target audience."

Technical SEO

Emma highlighted the significance of technical SEO in optimizing website performance. "Technical SEO involves optimizing the technical aspects of a website to improve its crawling, indexing, and overall search engine visibility," she explained. "It includes elements such as site speed, mobile-friendliness, crawlability, and site architecture."

David suggested conducting regular technical audits to identify and fix issues. "Technical audits help us identify areas for improvement and ensure our website is optimized for search engine crawlers," he noted. "Addressing technical issues promptly improves site performance and enhances user experience."

Lisa emphasized the importance of mobile optimization in today's digital landscape. "With the increasing use of mobile devices, mobile optimization is crucial for SEO success," she remarked. "We should ensure our website is mobile-friendly, loads quickly, and provides a seamless user experience across all devices."

Content Quality

Emma turned to the importance of content quality in SEO strategy. "Quality content is essential for attracting and retaining website visitors, earning backlinks, and improving search engine rankings," she explained. "It includes elements such as relevance, accuracy, comprehensiveness, and readability."

David suggested focusing on user intent when creating content. "Understanding user intent helps us create content that meets the needs and expectations of our target audience," he noted. "By addressing user intent effectively, we can improve engagement metrics and signal to search engines that our content is valuable."

Lisa emphasized the need for original, unique content. "Originality and uniqueness are key factors in content quality," she remarked. "We should strive to create content that offers fresh perspectives, insights, and value to our audience."

User Experience

Emma highlighted the importance of user experience in SEO strategy. "User experience plays a crucial role in determining how visitors interact with our website and whether they stay or leave," she explained. "It includes elements such as site navigation, page layout, readability, and visual appeal."

David suggested optimizing website usability for improved engagement. "A user-friendly website enhances engagement metrics such as time on site, pages per session, and bounce rate," he noted. "Improving website usability signals to search engines that our website provides a positive user experience."

Lisa emphasized the need for clear, intuitive navigation. "Clear, intuitive navigation helps visitors find what they're looking for quickly and easily," she remarked. "We should ensure our website navigation is simple, logical, and consistent across all pages."

Link Building

Emma turned to the importance of link building in SEO strategy. "Link building involves acquiring backlinks from other websites to our own," she explained. "Backlinks are a key ranking factor in search engine algorithms and signal to search engines that our website is authoritative and trustworthy."

David suggested focusing on earning quality backlinks from relevant, authoritative websites. "Quality backlinks from reputable websites carry more weight in search engine algorithms," he noted. "We should focus on building relationships with industry influencers, publishers, and bloggers to earn natural backlinks."

Lisa emphasized the need for a diversified link profile. "A diversified link profile with a mix of anchor texts, link types, and referring domains is essential for SEO success," she remarked. "We should focus on earning a variety of high-quality backlinks from diverse sources." As the meeting concluded, the room was filled with a sense of clarity and determination.

Paid Advertising Campaigns

In the vibrant conference room of InnovateTech, the team delved deeper into the realm of digital marketing, now focusing on the pivotal role of paid advertising campaigns. Lisa, Emma, David, and their colleagues understood that strategic use of paid advertising could amplify their reach, drive targeted traffic, and accelerate their business growth.

Lisa, the CEO, set the tone for the discussion with a determined tone. "Today, we explore the power of paid advertising campaigns in our digital marketing strategy," she declared. "Paid advertising offers us the opportunity to reach our target audience with precision and scale, driving meaningful results for our business."

David, the data guru, nodded in agreement. "Paid advertising campaigns allow us to target specific demographics, interests, and behaviors, ensuring that our message reaches the right audience at the right time," he explained. "By investing strategically in paid advertising, we can maximize our return on investment and achieve our business objectives."

Emma, the strategist, leaned forward with a plan. "Let's explore the key elements of successful paid advertising campaigns," she suggested. "We'll focus on six critical areas:

campaign objectives, audience targeting, ad creative, ad formats, budgeting, and performance tracking."

Lisa clicked her remote, and the projector displayed a comprehensive overview of paid advertising campaigns. "We'll start with campaign objectives," she said.

Campaign Objectives

Emma emphasized the importance of setting clear campaign objectives. "Campaign objectives define what we want to achieve with our paid advertising efforts," she explained. "Whether it's driving website traffic, generating leads, increasing sales, or raising brand awareness, clear objectives guide our strategy and measure our success."

David suggested aligning campaign objectives with broader business goals. "Our campaign objectives should support our overall business objectives," he noted. "By aligning our paid advertising efforts with business goals such as revenue growth or market expansion, we ensure that our campaigns deliver tangible results."

Lisa highlighted the need for SMART objectives—specific, measurable, achievable, relevant, and time-bound. "SMART objectives provide a framework for setting meaningful goals and tracking progress," she remarked. "They help us stay focused, motivated, and accountable throughout the campaign."

Audience Targeting

Emma turned to the importance of audience targeting in paid advertising campaigns. "Audience targeting allows us to reach the right people with the right message," she explained. "By defining our target audience based on demographics, interests, behaviors, and psychographics, we can ensure that our ads resonate with the intended audience."

David suggested leveraging data and analytics for audience segmentation. "Data-driven audience segmentation helps us identify and prioritize high-value audience segments," he noted. "By analyzing past campaign performance and customer data, we can refine our targeting criteria and optimize our ad spend."

Lisa emphasized the need for personalized messaging and creative for each audience segment. "Tailoring our ads to the specific needs, preferences, and pain points of each audience segment enhances relevance and engagement," she remarked. "Personalized ads resonate more deeply with the audience and drive better results."

Ad Creative

Emma highlighted the significance of compelling ad creative in paid advertising campaigns. "Ad creative is the heart and soul of our paid advertising efforts," she explained. "Eye-catching visuals, persuasive copy, and compelling calls-to-action capture attention, spark interest, and drive action."

David suggested testing different ad creative variations to optimize performance. "A/B testing allows us to compare different ad elements, such as headlines, images, and offers, to identify what resonates best with our audience," he noted. "Continuous testing and optimization ensure that our ad creative remains fresh, relevant, and effective."

Lisa emphasized the importance of storytelling in ad creative. "Storytelling evokes emotion, builds connections, and leaves a lasting impression on our audience," she remarked. "By weaving narratives into our ad creative, we can capture attention, foster engagement, and drive conversions."

Ad Formats

Emma turned to the variety of ad formats available in paid advertising campaigns. "Ad formats determine how our ads are displayed and interacted with across different channels and devices," she explained. "From text ads and display ads to video ads and social media ads, each ad format offers unique opportunities to engage our audience."

David suggested selecting ad formats based on campaign objectives and audience preferences. "Different ad formats are suitable for different campaign objectives and audience segments," he noted. "We should choose ad formats that align with our goals, resonate with our audience, and complement our ad creative."

Lisa highlighted the importance of mobile-friendly ad formats in today's mobile-first world. "With the majority of internet users accessing content on mobile devices, mobile-friendly ad formats are essential for reaching our audience effectively," she remarked. "We should ensure that our ad creative is optimized for mobile devices and delivers a seamless user experience across all screen sizes."

Budgeting

Emma emphasized the importance of budgeting in paid advertising campaigns. "Budgeting determines how much we invest in our paid advertising efforts and how we allocate our resources across different channels and campaigns," she explained. "By setting realistic budgets and monitoring our spending carefully, we can maximize our ROI and avoid overspending."

Social Media Optimization

As the sun cast warm hues through the windows of the InnovateTech conference room, the team gathered to explore the dynamic landscape of social media optimization. Lisa, Emma, David, and their colleagues understood the pivotal role of social media in connecting with their audience, building brand awareness, and driving engagement.

Lisa, the CEO, set the stage with a poised demeanor. "Today, we embark on a journey into the world of social media optimization," she declared. "Social media offers us a powerful platform to engage with our audience, share valuable content, and amplify our brand presence."

David, the data guru, nodded in agreement. "Social media optimization is essential for maximizing our reach, fostering community engagement, and driving meaningful interactions with our audience," he explained. "By optimizing our social media strategy, we can build stronger relationships with our customers and achieve our business objectives."

Emma, the strategist, leaned forward with a plan. "Let's dive into the key elements of successful social media optimization," she suggested. "We'll focus on six critical areas: profile optimization, content strategy, audience engagement, community management, hashtag strategy, and performance tracking."

Lisa clicked her remote, and the projector displayed a comprehensive overview of social media optimization. "We'll start with profile optimization," she said.

Profile Optimization

Emma emphasized the importance of profile optimization in social media strategy. "Social media profiles serve as our digital storefronts, representing our brand identity and values to the world," she explained. "By optimizing our profiles with accurate information, compelling visuals, and relevant keywords, we can make a strong first impression on our audience."

David suggested aligning profile information with brand messaging and values. "Consistency is key in profile optimization," he noted. "Our profile information, including bio, cover photo, and contact details, should reflect our brand identity and convey a clear value proposition to our audience."

Lisa highlighted the importance of visual branding in profile optimization. "Visual elements such as profile picture and cover photo are the first things users see when they visit our profiles," she remarked. "We should use high-quality images that represent our brand and create a memorable impression on our audience."

Content Strategy

Emma turned to the significance of content strategy in social media optimization. "Content is the currency of social media," she explained. "A well-defined content strategy ensures that we consistently deliver valuable, relevant, and engaging content to our audience, driving interactions and building brand loyalty."

David suggested diversifying content formats to keep the audience engaged. "Different content formats, such as images, videos, infographics, and stories, cater to different audience preferences and behaviors," he noted. "We should experiment with various content formats to identify what resonates best with our audience."

Lisa emphasized the need for a content calendar to maintain consistency and organization. "A content calendar helps us plan and schedule our social media content in advance," she remarked. "It ensures that we maintain a consistent posting schedule and cover a variety of topics that align with our audience's interests and needs."

Audience Engagement

Emma highlighted the importance of audience engagement in social media optimization. "Engagement is the lifeblood of social media," she explained. "By actively engaging with our audience through likes, comments, shares, and messages, we can foster meaningful interactions, build relationships, and strengthen brand loyalty."

David suggested using social listening tools to monitor conversations and sentiments around the brand. "Social listening allows us to track mentions, hashtags, and keywords related to our brand, industry, and competitors," he noted. "It provides valuable insights into our audience's preferences, pain points, and sentiment, helping us tailor our content and engagement strategy accordingly."

Lisa emphasized the need for authenticity and transparency in audience engagement. "Authenticity builds trust and credibility on social media," she remarked. "We should respond to comments and messages promptly, address customer inquiries and concerns openly, and show appreciation for our audience's support and feedback."

Community Management

Emma turned to the importance of community management in social media optimization. "Social media communities are a valuable asset for brands, providing a platform for customers to connect, share experiences, and support each other," she explained. "By nurturing and

engaging with our community members, we can cultivate brand advocates, drive word-of-mouth referrals, and create a positive brand image."

David suggested creating branded hashtags to encourage user-generated content and community participation. "Branded hashtags allow us to curate user-generated content and foster community engagement around specific themes or campaigns," he noted. "They help us amplify our brand message and build a sense of belonging among our audience."

Lisa emphasized the need for active moderation to maintain a positive and inclusive community environment. "Moderation ensures that our social media communities remain safe, respectful, and free from spam or inappropriate content," she remarked. "We should establish clear community guidelines and enforce them consistently to uphold our brand values and standards."

Hashtag Strategy

Emma highlighted the significance of hashtag strategy in social media optimization. "Hashtags are powerful tools for increasing discoverability, expanding reach, and joining conversations on social media," she explained. "By using relevant and trending hashtags strategically, we can make our content more visible to our target audience and attract new followers."

David suggested researching hashtags to identify relevant and popular ones in our industry or niche. "

Influencer Marketing

As sunlight streamed through the windows of the InnovateTech conference room, the team gathered to explore the realm of influencer marketing. Lisa, Emma, David, and their colleagues understood the potent impact of leveraging influencers to amplify their brand's reach, engage with their audience, and foster trust.

Lisa, the CEO, exuded confidence as she initiated the discussion. "Today, we delve into the world of influencer marketing, where the power of persuasion meets the prowess of social media," she declared. "Influencer marketing offers us a unique opportunity to connect with our audience through trusted voices, driving authentic engagement and advocacy for our brand."

David, the data guru, nodded in agreement. "Influencers wield significant influence over their dedicated followers, making them valuable partners in our marketing efforts," he explained. "By collaborating with influencers whose values align with ours, we can leverage their authenticity and credibility to enhance our brand's visibility and reputation."

Emma, the strategist, leaned forward with enthusiasm. "Let's uncover the secrets of successful influencer marketing," she suggested. "We'll focus on six critical areas: influencer identification, relationship building, campaign strategy, content collaboration, performance tracking, and ROI analysis."

Lisa clicked her remote, and the projector illuminated the room with a comprehensive overview of influencer marketing. "We'll start with influencer identification," she announced.

Influencer Identification

Emma emphasized the importance of strategic influencer identification in influencer marketing campaigns. "Influencer identification involves finding influencers whose audience demographics, interests, and values align with our brand," she explained. "By selecting influencers whose followers match our target audience, we can ensure that our message resonates authentically with the right people."

David suggested leveraging influencer discovery tools and platforms to identify potential partners. "Influencer discovery tools provide valuable insights into influencers' reach, engagement, audience demographics, and brand affiliations," he noted. "They help us identify influencers who have the potential to drive meaningful results for our brand."

Lisa highlighted the need for thorough vetting and due diligence when selecting influencers. "We should evaluate influencers based on their authenticity, credibility, relevance, and alignment with our brand values," she remarked. "Choosing the right influencers is essential for building trust with our audience and achieving our campaign objectives."

Relationship Building

Emma turned to the significance of relationship building in influencer marketing. "Building strong relationships with influencers is key to successful collaboration," she explained. "By fostering genuine connections and mutual respect, we can establish long-term partnerships that yield meaningful results for both parties."

David suggested engaging with influencers authentically and respectfully. "We should approach influencers as partners, not just as marketing assets," he noted. "Taking the time to understand their interests, preferences, and goals can help us build rapport and trust, laying the foundation for fruitful collaboration."

Lisa emphasized the importance of clear communication and transparency in influencer relationships. "Open and honest communication is essential for aligning expectations, defining objectives, and ensuring a smooth collaboration process," she remarked. "We should establish clear guidelines, timelines, and deliverables to set the stage for a successful partnership."

Campaign Strategy

Emma highlighted the significance of strategic campaign planning in influencer marketing. "Campaign strategy involves defining campaign objectives, messaging, creative direction, and KPIs," she explained. "By aligning our campaign strategy with our overall marketing goals, we can ensure that our influencer collaborations deliver tangible results for our brand."

David suggested tailoring campaign strategies to fit each influencer's strengths and audience preferences. "Every influencer is unique, with their own voice, style, and content preferences," he noted. "We should customize our campaign strategy to leverage each influencer's strengths and maximize their impact on their audience."

Lisa emphasized the need for authenticity and creativity in campaign execution. "Authenticity is key in influencer marketing," she remarked. "Our campaigns should feel genuine and organic, aligning seamlessly with the influencer's content and audience expectations."

Content Collaboration

Emma turned to the importance of content collaboration in influencer marketing. "Content collaboration involves co-creating content with influencers that resonates with their audience and reinforces our brand message," she explained. "By involving influencers in the content creation process, we can ensure that our message is communicated authentically and effectively."

David suggested providing influencers with creative freedom while maintaining brand consistency. "We should empower influencers to express themselves authentically while providing guidance and direction to ensure brand alignment," he noted. "A collaborative approach allows us to leverage influencers' creativity and expertise while maintaining control over our brand message."

Lisa emphasized the value of storytelling and narrative

in content collaboration. "Storytelling is a powerful tool for connecting with audiences on an emotional level," she remarked. "Our content should tell a compelling story that resonates with the influencer's audience and reinforces our brand values and messaging."

As the meeting concluded, the room was filled with a sense of excitement and anticipation. The team at InnovateTech understood that influencer marketing offered a unique opportunity to connect with their audience in a meaningful way. With a strategic approach to influencer identification, relationship building, campaign planning, and content collaboration, they were poised to leverage the power of influencers to elevate their brand and achieve their marketing objectives.

Webinars and Virtual Events

In the vibrant atmosphere of the InnovateTech conference room, the team eagerly delved into the realm of webinars and virtual events. Lisa, Emma, David, and their colleagues understood the significance of leveraging these digital platforms to engage with their audience, share valuable insights, and drive meaningful interactions.

Lisa, the CEO, exuded confidence as she initiated the discussion. "Today, we explore the dynamic world of webinars and virtual events, where knowledge meets technology to create immersive experiences for our audience," she declared. "Webinars and virtual events offer us a unique opportunity to connect with our audience in real-time, deliver valuable content, and foster meaningful engagement."

David, the data guru, nodded in agreement. "Webinars and virtual events provide a platform for interactive communication, allowing us to educate, inspire, and connect with our audience on a deeper level," he explained. "By leveraging these digital platforms strategically, we can create memorable experiences that drive brand awareness, loyalty, and advocacy."

Emma, the strategist, leaned forward with enthusiasm. "Let's uncover the secrets of successful webinars and virtual events," she suggested. "We'll focus on six critical areas: event planning, content creation, audience engagement, technical execution, performance tracking, and post-event follow-up."

Lisa clicked her remote, and the projector illuminated the room with a comprehensive overview of webinars and virtual events. "We'll start with event planning," she announced.

Event Planning

Emma emphasized the importance of strategic event planning in hosting successful webinars and virtual events. "Event planning involves defining event objectives, selecting topics, scheduling, promoting, and coordinating logistics," she explained. "By carefully planning each aspect of our event, we can ensure a seamless and engaging experience for our audience."

David suggested aligning event topics with audience interests and needs. "Our event topics should address relevant industry trends, challenges, and opportunities that resonate with our audience," he noted. "By selecting compelling topics that offer valuable insights and solutions, we can attract and retain audience interest."

Lisa highlighted the importance of promoting events through various channels to maximize reach and participation.

"Promotion is key to driving attendance and engagement for our webinars and virtual events," she remarked. "We should leverage email marketing, social media, website announcements, and partnerships to spread the word and generate excitement."

Content Creation

Emma turned to the significance of content creation in webinar and virtual event success. "Content is the cornerstone of our events, providing value and relevance to our audience," she explained. "By creating compelling presentations, interactive sessions, and engaging discussions, we can capture audience attention and deliver meaningful insights."

David suggested involving subject matter experts and thought leaders in content creation to provide diverse perspectives and expertise. "Collaborating with industry experts adds credibility and depth to our event content," he noted. "By featuring guest speakers, panel discussions, and Q&A sessions, we can enrich the content and provide valuable insights to our audience."

Lisa emphasized the importance of storytelling and narrative in content creation. "Storytelling captivates audience attention and creates an emotional connection," she remarked. "Our content should tell a compelling story that resonates with our audience, addresses their pain points, and inspires action."

Audience Engagement

Emma highlighted the significance of audience engagement in webinar and virtual event success. "Audience engagement drives participation, interaction, and retention," she explained. "By incorporating interactive elements such as polls, quizzes, chats, and Q&A sessions, we can keep our audience engaged and actively involved in the event."

David suggested encouraging audience participation through gamification and incentives. "Gamification adds an element of fun and competition to our events, motivating participants to engage more actively," he noted. "By offering incentives such as prizes, discounts, or exclusive content, we can incentivize participation and reward audience engagement."

Lisa emphasized the importance of responsiveness and interaction during the event. "We should actively engage with our audience, respond to their questions and comments, and encourage open dialogue," she remarked. "Creating a participatory environment fosters a sense of community and connection among attendees."

Technical Execution

Emma turned to the importance of technical execution in webinar and virtual event success. "Technical execution involves selecting the right platform, testing equipment, setting up the event environment, and managing technical issues," she explained. "By ensuring a smooth and seamless technical experience, we can minimize disruptions and create a positive impression on our audience."

David suggested conducting thorough rehearsals and technical checks before the event to identify and address any potential issues. "Rehearsals help us familiarize ourselves with the event flow, test equipment and software, and troubleshoot any technical issues," he noted. "By rehearsing diligently, we can minimize technical glitches and ensure a flawless event execution."

Lisa highlighted the importance of contingency planning for technical issues or emergencies. "We should have backup plans and resources in place to address any unexpected technical challenges," she remarked. "Being prepared for contingencies allows us to handle issues swiftly and minimize disruptions to the event."

As the meeting concluded, the room was filled with a sense of anticipation and excitement. The team at InnovateTech understood that hosting successful webinars and virtual events required careful planning, engaging content, seamless technical execution, and active audience participation. With a strategic approach to event planning, content creation, audience engagement, and technical execution, they were poised to create memorable experiences that drive brand awareness, engagement, and loyalty.

Analytics for Digital Campaigns

In the dynamic setting of the InnovateTech conference room, the team delved into the critical aspect of analytics for digital campaigns. Lisa, Emma, David, and their colleagues understood the pivotal role of data-driven insights in optimizing their digital marketing efforts, refining strategies, and driving meaningful results.

Lisa, the CEO, exuded confidence as she initiated the discussion. "Today, we explore the transformative power of analytics for digital campaigns, where data illuminates the path to success," she declared. "Analytics provide us with valuable insights into the performance of our campaigns, helping us understand what works, what doesn't, and how we can improve our strategies to achieve our objectives."

David, the data guru, nodded in agreement. "Analytics enable us to measure, track, and analyze key performance metrics, allowing us to make informed decisions and optimize our digital marketing efforts," he explained. "By leveraging data effectively, we can identify trends, patterns, and opportunities that drive business growth and competitive advantage."

Emma, the strategist, leaned forward with enthusiasm. "Let's unlock the secrets of successful analytics for digital campaigns," she suggested. "We'll focus on six critical areas: data collection, metrics definition, performance analysis, optimization strategies, reporting, and continuous improvement."

Lisa clicked her remote, and the projector illuminated the room with a comprehensive overview of analytics for digital campaigns. "We'll start with data collection," she announced.

Data Collection

Emma emphasized the importance of robust data collection processes in gathering accurate and reliable data for analysis. "Data collection involves capturing relevant data points from various sources, including website analytics, social media platforms, email marketing tools, and advertising platforms," she explained. "By collecting comprehensive data sets, we can gain a holistic view of our digital marketing performance and audience behavior."

David suggested implementing tracking mechanisms such as pixels, cookies, and tags to capture user interactions and behavior across digital channels. "Tracking mechanisms allow us to collect data on user interactions, such as website visits, page views, clicks, conversions, and engagement metrics," he noted. "By deploying tracking mechanisms effectively, we can capture granular data that informs our decision-making and optimization efforts."

Lisa highlighted the importance of data privacy and compliance in data collection processes. "We must prioritize data privacy and compliance with regulations such as GDPR and CCPA," she remarked. "By obtaining consent, anonymizing data, and adhering to best practices in data handling, we can build trust with our audience and protect their privacy rights."

Metrics Definition

Emma turned to the significance of defining relevant metrics that align with campaign objectives and business goals. "Metrics definition involves selecting key performance indicators (KPIs) that measure the success of our digital campaigns," she explained. "By choosing metrics that are specific, measurable, achievable, relevant, and time-bound (SMART), we can track progress and evaluate performance effectively."

David suggested aligning metrics with each stage of the customer journey to gain insights into the effectiveness of marketing efforts at each touchpoint. "Metrics such as traffic sources, conversion rates, customer acquisition costs, and lifetime value provide valuable insights into the customer journey," he noted. "By analyzing metrics at each stage, we can identify opportunities for optimization and improvement."

Lisa emphasized the importance of focusing on meaningful metrics that drive actionable insights and inform decision-making. "We should prioritize metrics that directly impact our business objectives, such as revenue, ROI, customer acquisition, retention, and engagement," she remarked. "By focusing on actionable metrics, we can allocate resources effectively and drive meaningful results for our business."

Performance Analysis

Emma highlighted the significance of conducting thorough performance analysis to evaluate the effectiveness of digital campaigns. "Performance analysis involves analyzing data, identifying trends, patterns, and insights, and deriving actionable insights to inform decision-making and optimization strategies," she explained. "By conducting regular performance analysis, we can identify strengths, weaknesses, opportunities, and threats to our campaigns and adjust our strategies accordingly."

David suggested using data visualization tools and dashboards to present insights in a clear, concise, and actionable manner. "Data visualization tools such as charts, graphs, and dashboards help us visualize complex data sets and identify trends and patterns at a glance," he noted. "By presenting insights visually, we can communicate findings more effectively and facilitate data-driven decision-making."

Lisa emphasized the importance of conducting comparative analysis to benchmark performance against industry standards, competitors, and historical data. "Comparative analysis provides context and perspective to our performance metrics," she remarked. "By comparing our performance against benchmarks and competitors, we can identify areas of strength and weakness and prioritize optimization efforts accordingly."

Optimization Strategies

Emma turned to the significance of optimization strategies in maximizing the effectiveness of digital campaigns based on data insights. "Optimization strategies involve making data-driven adjustments to campaign elements such as targeting, messaging, creative, timing, and budget allocation to improve performance and achieve objectives," she explained. "By iterating and refining our campaigns based on data insights, we can optimize results and drive continuous improvement."

David suggested implementing A/B testing and multivariate testing to experiment with different variables and identify the most effective combinations. "A/B testing allows us to compare two versions of a campaign element, such as ad copy or landing page design, to determine which performs better," he noted. "Multivariate testing extends this concept by testing multiple variables simultaneously to identify the optimal combination."

Lisa highlighted the importance of iterative optimization based on ongoing performance analysis and testing. "Optimization is an ongoing process that requires continuous monitoring, testing, and refinement," she remarked. "By iterating and optimizing our campaigns based on real-time data insights, we can stay agile, adaptive, and responsive to changes in the market and audience behavior."

Reporting

Emma emphasized the significance of comprehensive and insightful reporting to communicate campaign performance and insights effectively. "Reporting involves synthesizing data, analyzing trends, and summarizing key findings in clear, concise, and actionable reports," she explained. "By presenting insights in an accessible format, we can facilitate decision-making, foster alignment, and drive accountability across the organization."

David suggested tailoring reports to the needs and preferences of different stakeholders, such as executives, marketers, and sales teams. "Different stakeholders have different information needs and priorities," he noted. "By customizing reports to address specific questions and objectives, we can ensure that each stakeholder receives relevant and actionable insights."

Lisa highlighted the importance of using reports to celebrate successes, recognize achievements, and identify areas for improvement. "Reports provide an opportunity to celebrate wins, acknowledge contributions, and learn from mistakes," she remarked. "By fostering a culture of transparency, accountability, and continuous learning, we can drive continuous improvement and innovation."

Continuous Improvement

Emma turned to the significance of embracing a culture of continuous improvement in digital marketing efforts. "Continuous improvement involves learning from past experiences, experimenting with new approaches, and adapting strategies based on feedback and insights," she explained. "By fostering a culture of curiosity, experimentation, and innovation, we can stay ahead of the curve and drive sustained growth and success."

David suggested conducting post-campaign reviews and retrospectives to reflect on successes, challenges, and lessons learned. "Post-campaign reviews provide an opportunity to evaluate performance, identify areas for improvement, and capture insights for future campaigns," he noted. "By conducting thorough retrospectives, we can extract valuable learnings and apply them to future initiatives."

11

Chapter 11: Enhancing Customer Experience

Understanding Customer Journey Mapping

In the bustling atmosphere of the InnovateTech conference room, the team gathered to embark on a journey into the realm of enhancing customer experience. Lisa, Emma, David, and their colleagues understood the profound impact of understanding customer journey mapping in delivering exceptional experiences that resonate with their audience.

Lisa, the CEO, exuded confidence as she initiated the discussion. "Today, we explore the art and science of customer journey mapping, where empathy meets strategy to create memorable experiences for our customers," she declared. "Customer journey mapping offers us a holistic view of our customers' interactions with our brand, helping us identify pain points, moments of delight, and opportunities for improvement."

David, the data guru, nodded in agreement. "Customer journey mapping enables us to walk in our customers' shoes, understanding their needs, preferences, and behaviors at each stage of their interaction with our brand," he explained. "By mapping the customer journey, we can identify touchpoints, channels, and interactions that shape the overall experience and drive customer satisfaction and loyalty."

Emma, the strategist, leaned forward with enthusiasm. "Let's unravel the mysteries of successful customer journey mapping," she suggested. "We'll focus on six critical areas: defining the customer journey, identifying touchpoints, understanding customer emotions, addressing pain points, fostering moments of delight, and continuous optimization."

Lisa clicked her remote, and the projector illuminated the room with a comprehensive overview of customer journey mapping. "We'll start with defining the customer journey," she announced.

Defining the Customer Journey

Emma emphasized the importance of defining the customer journey to understand the end-to-end experience from the customer's perspective. "The customer journey represents the series of interactions and touchpoints that a customer experiences from initial awareness to post-purchase support," she explained. "By defining the stages of the customer journey, we can map out the key milestones and touchpoints that shape the overall experience."

David suggested aligning the customer journey with business objectives and customer goals. "The customer journey should reflect the customer's goals, motivations, and expectations at each stage of their interaction with our brand," he noted. "By aligning the customer journey with our business objectives, we can ensure that our efforts are focused on delivering value and meeting customer needs."

Lisa highlighted the importance of cross-functional collaboration in defining the customer journey. "The customer journey cuts across various departments and functions within our organization, including marketing, sales, customer service, and product development," she remarked. "By involving stakeholders from different departments, we can gain diverse perspectives and ensure that the customer journey reflects the end-to-end experience."

As the discussion unfolded, the team delved deeper into the intricacies of customer journey mapping, recognizing its significance in shaping the overall customer experience. With a strategic approach to defining the customer journey, they were poised to unlock new insights, identify opportunities for improvement, and deliver exceptional experiences that delight their customers at every touchpoint.

Creating Seamless Omnichannel Experiences

In the innovative setting of the InnovateTech conference room, the team delved into the complexities of creating seamless omnichannel experiences. Lisa, Emma, David, and their colleagues understood the pivotal role of omnichannel strategies in delivering cohesive and integrated experiences that transcend individual channels.

Lisa, the CEO, exuded confidence as she initiated the discussion. "Today, we explore the art of creating seamless omnichannel experiences, where consistency meets convenience to elevate the customer journey," she declared. "Omnichannel experiences offer us the opportunity to connect with our customers seamlessly across multiple touchpoints, channels, and devices, providing a unified and cohesive experience."

David, the data guru, nodded in agreement. "Omnichannel strategies enable us to meet our customers wherever they are, providing a consistent and integrated experience across online and offline channels," he explained. "By leveraging data and technology, we can ensure that our customers enjoy a seamless journey, regardless of how they choose to interact with our brand."

Emma, the strategist, leaned forward with enthusiasm. "Let's unravel the complexities of creating seamless omnichannel experiences," she suggested. "We'll focus on six critical areas: channel integration, data synchronization, personalized interactions, consistent messaging, frictionless transactions, and continuous optimization."

Lisa clicked her remote, and the projector illuminated the room with a comprehensive overview of omnichannel experiences. "We'll start with channel integration," she announced.

Channel Integration

Emma emphasized the importance of integrating channels to provide a cohesive and connected experience for customers. "Channel integration involves aligning our online and offline channels to create a seamless journey for customers," she explained. "By breaking down silos and connecting channels such as websites, mobile apps, social media, email, and physical stores, we can ensure that customers can move effortlessly between channels without any disruption."

David suggested leveraging technology such as customer relationship management (CRM) systems and marketing automation platforms to integrate data and interactions across channels. "Technology plays a crucial role in channel integration, allowing us to capture, analyze, and synchronize customer data and interactions in real-time," he noted. "By leveraging CRM systems and marketing automation platforms, we can track customer interactions, preferences, and behaviors across channels, enabling personalized and contextually relevant experiences."

Lisa highlighted the importance of consistency in branding, messaging, and user experience across channels. "Consistency is key to creating a seamless omnichannel experience," she remarked. "Our branding, messaging, and user experience should remain consistent across all touchpoints, ensuring that customers receive a unified and cohesive experience regardless of the channel they choose to interact with."

As the discussion progressed, the team explored the intricacies of channel integration, recognizing its significance in delivering seamless omnichannel experiences. With a strategic approach to integrating channels, they were poised to break down silos, leverage technology, and deliver cohesive experiences that delight customers across every touchpoint.

Personalization Tactics

In the vibrant atmosphere of the InnovateTech conference room, the team delved into the intricacies of personalization tactics. Lisa, Emma, David, and their colleagues understood the transformative power of personalization in creating meaningful and tailored experiences for their customers.

Lisa, the CEO, exuded confidence as she initiated the discussion. "Today, we explore the art of personalization tactics, where data meets empathy to create experiences that resonate with our customers on a personal level," she declared. "Personalization offers us the opportunity to connect with our customers in a meaningful way, delivering relevant content, recommendations, and interactions that cater to their unique preferences and needs."

David, the data guru, nodded in agreement. "Personalization tactics enable us to leverage customer data and insights to deliver tailored experiences across various touchpoints and channels," he explained. "By understanding our customers' preferences, behaviors, and interests, we can deliver personalized content, recommendations, and offers that resonate with their individual needs and preferences."

Emma, the strategist, leaned forward with enthusiasm. "Let's uncover the secrets of successful personalization tactics," she suggested. "We'll focus on six critical areas: data collection, segmentation, targeting, content personalization, recommendation engines, and predictive analytics."

Lisa clicked her remote, and the projector illuminated the room with a comprehensive overview of personalization tactics. "We'll start with data collection," she announced.

Data Collection

Emma emphasized the importance of robust data collection processes in gathering the insights needed for personalization. "Data collection involves capturing and analyzing customer data from various sources, including websites, mobile apps,

CRM systems, and third-party sources," she explained. "By collecting comprehensive data sets, we can gain insights into customer preferences, behaviors, and interactions that inform our personalization efforts."

David suggested leveraging technologies such as customer data platforms (CDPs) and data management platforms (DMPs) to aggregate and unify customer data from disparate sources. "CDPs and DMPs enable us to centralize and integrate customer data from multiple sources, providing a single view of the customer," he noted. "By consolidating customer data, we can gain a holistic understanding of each customer's journey and preferences."

Lisa highlighted the importance of data privacy and compliance in data collection processes. "Data privacy is paramount in personalization efforts," she remarked. "We must prioritize data privacy and comply with regulations such as GDPR and CCPA, ensuring that customer data is collected and used ethically and transparently."

As the discussion unfolded, the team delved deeper into the intricacies of personalization tactics, recognizing their significance in delivering tailored experiences that resonate with customers. With a strategic approach to data collection, segmentation, targeting, and content personalization, they were poised to unlock new insights, drive engagement, and foster loyalty through personalized interactions across every touchpoint.

Improving Customer Support

In the lively ambiance of the InnovateTech conference room, the team delved into the vital aspect of improving customer support. Lisa, Emma, David, and their colleagues recognized the paramount importance of providing exceptional support to ensure customer satisfaction and loyalty.

Lisa, the CEO, initiated the discussion with enthusiasm. "Today, we explore the realm of improving customer support, where empathy meets efficiency to address our customers' needs and concerns," she declared. "Exceptional customer support is the cornerstone of our commitment to customer-centricity, and it plays a pivotal role in shaping the overall customer experience."

David, the data guru, nodded in agreement. "Improving customer support involves leveraging data and technology to deliver timely, personalized, and effective assistance to our customers," he explained. "By understanding our customers' needs and preferences, we can tailor our support efforts to meet their expectations and resolve issues efficiently."

Emma, the strategist, leaned forward with determination. "Let's uncover the strategies for enhancing customer support," she suggested. "We'll focus on six critical areas: omnichannel support, self-service options, proactive support, personalized interactions, continuous training, and performance monitoring."

Lisa clicked her remote, and the projector illuminated the room with a comprehensive overview of improving customer support. "We'll start with omnichannel support," she announced.

Omnichannel Support

Emma emphasized the importance of offering support across multiple channels to meet customers where they are. "Omnichannel support ensures that customers can reach out for assistance through their preferred channels, whether it's phone, email, chat, social media, or in-person," she explained. "By providing a seamless experience across channels, we can make it easier for customers to get the help they need, whenever and wherever they need it."

David suggested integrating customer support channels and data to provide a consistent experience across touchpoints. "Integrating support channels allows us to capture and track customer interactions and data in a centralized system," he noted. "By unifying customer data and interactions, we can provide agents with a complete view of the customer's history and context, enabling personalized and efficient support."

Lisa highlighted the importance of empowering customers with self-service options to find answers to their questions independently. "Self-service options such as knowledge bases, FAQs, tutorials, and chatbots enable customers to resolve common issues on their own," she remarked. "By offering self-service options, we can reduce the burden on support agents and empower customers to find solutions quickly and easily."

As the discussion continued, the team explored the intricacies of improving customer support, recognizing its significance in driving customer satisfaction, loyalty, and advocacy. With a strategic approach to omnichannel support, self-service options, proactive assistance, and continuous training, they were poised to elevate the support experience and delight customers at every touchpoint.

Collecting and Acting on Feedback

In the bustling atmosphere of the InnovateTech conference room, the team delved into the crucial aspect of collecting and acting on feedback. Lisa, Emma, David, and their colleagues understood the invaluable insights feedback provides in refining their customer experience strategies.

Lisa, the CEO, initiated the discussion with a sense of purpose. "Today, we explore the significance of collecting and acting on feedback, where insights from our customers guide us in shaping exceptional experiences," she declared. "Feedback is the voice of our customers, offering us valuable insights into their needs, preferences, and expectations."

David, the data guru, nodded in agreement. "Collecting and acting on feedback enables us to understand our customers' perceptions and sentiments, identify areas for improvement, and drive meaningful change," he explained. "By listening to our customers, we can foster a culture of continuous improvement and innovation."

Emma, the strategist, leaned forward with anticipation. "Let's unravel the strategies for collecting and acting on feedback," she suggested. "We'll focus on six critical areas: feedback channels, surveys and polls, sentiment analysis, feedback loops, action planning, and communication."

Lisa clicked her remote, and the projector illuminated the room with a comprehensive overview of collecting and acting on feedback. "We'll start with feedback channels," she announced.

Feedback Channels

Emma emphasized the importance of offering multiple channels for customers to provide feedback. "Feedback channels should be accessible and convenient for customers to share their thoughts and experiences," she explained. "Whether it's through surveys, email, social media, or in-person interactions, we must provide avenues for customers to voice their opinions."

David suggested leveraging technology to capture feedback in real-time across various touchpoints. "Technology enables us to collect feedback efficiently and effectively," he noted. "By using tools such as feedback widgets, chatbots, and sentiment analysis software, we can capture feedback in real-time and gain insights into customer sentiment and satisfaction."

Lisa highlighted the significance of actively listening to customer feedback and acknowledging their input. "Listening to our customers is the first step, but we must also show that we value their feedback and take it seriously," she remarked. "By responding promptly and transparently to feedback, we can build trust and credibility with our customers."

As the discussion unfolded, the team explored the intricacies of collecting and acting on feedback, recognizing its pivotal role in driving customer-centricity and continuous improvement. With a strategic approach to feedback channels, surveys and polls, sentiment analysis, feedback loops, action planning, and communication, they were poised to harness the power of customer insights to shape exceptional experiences and foster lasting relationships.

Building Customer Loyalty Programs

In the dynamic setting of the InnovateTech conference room, the team delved into the strategic aspect of building customer loyalty programs. Lisa, Emma, David, and their colleagues recognized the pivotal role of loyalty programs in fostering lasting relationships and driving customer retention.

Lisa, the CEO, initiated the discussion with enthusiasm. "Today, we explore the art of building customer loyalty programs, where rewards meet recognition to cultivate loyalty and advocacy," she declared. "Loyalty programs offer us the opportunity to incentivize and reward our customers for their continued support, encouraging repeat purchases and fostering brand loyalty."

David, the data guru, nodded in agreement. "Building customer loyalty programs involves leveraging data and insights to design personalized and compelling incentives that resonate with our customers," he explained. "By understanding our customers' preferences and behaviors, we can tailor loyalty programs to meet their needs and drive engagement and retention."

Emma, the strategist, leaned forward with determination. "Let's uncover the strategies for building customer loyalty programs," she suggested. "We'll focus on six critical areas: program design, rewards structure, tiered benefits, personalized offers, engagement tactics, and performance measurement."

Lisa clicked her remote, and the projector illuminated the room with a comprehensive overview of building customer loyalty programs. "We'll start with program design," she announced.

Program Design

Emma emphasized the importance of designing loyalty programs that align with the brand values and customer expectations. "Program design involves defining the structure, rules, and benefits of the loyalty program," she explained. "By offering a clear value proposition and intuitive user experience, we can encourage customers to enroll and participate in the program."

David suggested leveraging data to segment customers and tailor loyalty program offerings to their preferences and behaviors. "Personalization is key to the success of loyalty programs," he noted. "By analyzing customer data and insights, we can segment customers based on their spending habits, preferences, and loyalty status, and offer personalized rewards and incentives that resonate with each segment."

Lisa highlighted the importance of transparency and simplicity in loyalty program design. "Customers appreciate transparency and simplicity in loyalty programs," she remarked. "We must clearly communicate the program benefits, terms, and conditions to ensure that customers understand how they can earn and redeem rewards."

As the discussion continued, the team explored the intricacies of building customer loyalty programs, recognizing their significance in driving repeat purchases, engagement, and advocacy. With a strategic approach to program design, rewards structure, personalized offers, and engagement tactics, they were poised to cultivate loyal and enthusiastic customers who would champion their brand and contribute to its long-term success.

12

Chapter 12: Sales and Marketing Automation

Benefits of Automation

In the innovative atmosphere of the InnovateTech conference room, the team delved into the transformative power of sales and marketing automation. Lisa, Emma, David, and their colleagues recognized the pivotal role of automation in streamlining processes, driving efficiency, and enhancing productivity.

Lisa, the CEO, initiated the discussion with enthusiasm. "Today, we explore the myriad benefits of sales and marketing automation, where technology meets efficiency to propel our business forward," she declared. "Automation offers us the opportunity to automate repetitive tasks, streamline workflows, and optimize resource allocation, enabling us to focus our efforts on high-value activities and strategic initiatives."

David, the data guru, nodded in agreement. "Sales and

marketing automation empowers us to leverage technology to scale our efforts, reach our target audience more effectively, and drive engagement and conversions," he explained. "By automating routine tasks such as lead nurturing, email marketing, and data analysis, we can free up time and resources to focus on building relationships and driving revenue."

Emma, the strategist, leaned forward with anticipation. "Let's uncover the advantages of sales and marketing automation," she suggested. "We'll focus on six critical areas: efficiency gains, scalability, consistency, data-driven insights, lead management, and customer engagement."

Lisa clicked her remote, and the projector illuminated the room with a comprehensive overview of the benefits of automation. "We'll start with efficiency gains," she announced.

Efficiency Gains

Emma emphasized the transformative impact of automation on productivity and efficiency. "Automation enables us to streamline processes and eliminate manual tasks, reducing the time and effort required to complete them," she explained. "By automating routine activities such as data entry, lead scoring, and report generation, we can save valuable time and resources, allowing our teams to focus on higher-value tasks and strategic initiatives."

David suggested that automation could also enhance accuracy and reduce errors in repetitive tasks. "Automation reduces the risk of human error and ensures consistency and accuracy in our processes," he noted. "By automating data entry, for example, we can minimize the likelihood of errors and ensure that our data is clean, accurate, and up-to-date, enabling us to make informed decisions and drive results."

Lisa highlighted the scalability of automation, allowing businesses to handle increasing volumes of work without significantly increasing resources. "Automation enables us to scale our efforts and operations to meet growing demand and business needs," she remarked. "As our business expands, automation allows us to efficiently manage larger volumes of leads, customers, and transactions, ensuring that we can continue to deliver exceptional experiences and drive growth."

As the discussion continued, the team explored the myriad benefits of sales and marketing automation, recognizing its transformative impact on productivity, efficiency, and scalability. With a strategic approach to automation, they were poised to harness the power of technology to drive innovation, streamline processes, and achieve their business objectives.

Choosing the Right Tools

In the vibrant ambiance of the InnovateTech conference room, the team delved into the crucial aspect of selecting the right tools for sales and marketing automation. Lisa, Emma, David, and their colleagues understood the significance of choosing the tools that best fit their business needs and objectives.

Lisa, the CEO, initiated the discussion with purpose. "Today, we explore the importance of choosing the right tools for sales and marketing automation, where technology meets strategy to drive success," she declared. "Selecting the right tools is essential in maximizing the benefits of automation and achieving our business goals."

David, the data guru, nodded in agreement. "Choosing the right tools involves evaluating our requirements, assessing available options, and selecting solutions that align with our business needs, budget, and technical capabilities," he explained. "By selecting the right tools, we can ensure seamless integration, scalability, and efficiency in our automation efforts."

Emma, the strategist, leaned forward with determination. "Let's uncover the strategies for choosing the right tools," she suggested. "We'll focus on six critical areas: defining requirements, conducting research, evaluating options, considering integration, assessing scalability, and calculating ROI."

Lisa clicked her remote, and the projector illuminated the room with a comprehensive overview of choosing the right tools. "We'll start with defining requirements," she announced.

Defining Requirements

Emma emphasized the importance of identifying and prioritizing the features and functionalities needed to support sales and marketing automation initiatives. "Defining requirements involves understanding our business needs, objectives, and workflows," she explained. "By clearly defining our requirements, we can narrow down our options and focus on solutions that offer the features and capabilities we need to achieve our goals."

David suggested involving key stakeholders from sales, marketing, IT, and other relevant departments in the requirements gathering process. "Collaboration is key to identifying requirements that meet the needs of all stakeholders," he noted. "By involving stakeholders from different departments, we can gain diverse perspectives and ensure that the selected tools align with the needs and objectives of the entire organization."

Lisa highlighted the importance of flexibility and scalability in selecting tools that can grow and adapt with the business. "Scalability is essential in future-proofing our automation efforts," she remarked. "We must select tools that can scale with our business and accommodate future growth and expansion."

As the discussion continued, the team explored the intricacies of choosing the right tools for sales and marketing automation, recognizing its significance in driving efficiency, effectiveness, and success. With a strategic approach to defining requirements, conducting research, and evaluating options, they were poised to select tools that would empower them to achieve their business objectives and drive growth.

Implementing CRM Systems

In the focused environment of the InnovateTech conference room, the team delved into the pivotal aspect of implementing CRM (Customer Relationship Management) systems for sales and marketing automation. Lisa, Emma, David, and their colleagues understood the transformative potential of CRM systems in managing customer relationships and driving business growth.

Lisa, the CEO, set the tone for the discussion with determination. "Today, we explore the implementation of CRM systems, where technology meets relationship-building to propel our business forward," she declared. "Implementing CRM systems allows us to centralize customer data, streamline processes, and optimize interactions, enabling us to deliver personalized and seamless experiences across every touchpoint."

David, the data guru, nodded in agreement. "CRM systems serve as the backbone of our sales and marketing operations, providing a unified platform for managing leads, contacts, opportunities, and campaigns," he explained. "By implementing CRM systems, we can gain insights into customer behaviors, preferences, and interactions, empowering us to make data-driven decisions and drive results."

Emma, the strategist, leaned forward with anticipation. "Let's uncover the strategies for implementing CRM systems," she suggested. "We'll focus on six critical areas: planning and preparation, data migration, customization and configuration, user training, adoption strategies, and ongoing support."

Lisa clicked her remote, and the projector illuminated the room with a comprehensive overview of implementing CRM systems. "We'll start with planning and preparation," she announced.

Planning and Preparation

Emma emphasized the importance of thorough planning and preparation in ensuring a successful CRM implementation. "Planning and preparation involve defining objectives, identifying stakeholders, and creating a roadmap for implementation," she explained. "By establishing clear goals and milestones, we can align our CRM implementation efforts with our business objectives and ensure a smooth transition."

David suggested conducting a comprehensive assessment of existing data and processes to identify gaps and opportunities for improvement. "Data migration is a critical aspect of CRM implementation," he noted. "By assessing existing data quality, completeness, and relevance, we can develop a data migration strategy that ensures the accuracy and integrity of our customer data in the CRM system."

Lisa highlighted the significance of customization and configuration in tailoring the CRM system to meet the specific needs and workflows of the organization. "Customization and configuration allow us to adapt the CRM system to our unique business requirements," she remarked. "By configuring fields, layouts, and workflows, we can ensure that the CRM system aligns with our processes and enables our teams to work more efficiently."

As the discussion continued, the team explored the intricacies of implementing CRM systems, recognizing its significance in centralizing data, streamlining processes, and enhancing customer relationships. With a strategic approach to planning and preparation, data migration, customization and configuration, they were poised to leverage CRM systems to drive efficiency, effectiveness, and success in their sales and marketing efforts.

Automating Lead Nurturing

In the focused environment of the InnovateTech conference room, the team delved into the critical aspect of automating lead nurturing. Lisa, Emma, David, and their colleagues understood the pivotal role of lead nurturing in building relationships and driving conversions.

Lisa, the CEO, set the stage for the discussion with determination. "Today, we explore the automation of lead nurturing, where technology meets engagement to guide prospects through the buyer's journey," she declared. "Automating lead nurturing allows us to deliver timely, relevant, and personalized content to prospects, nurturing them from initial interest to conversion."

David, the data guru, nodded in agreement. "Lead nurturing involves engaging prospects with targeted content and interactions at each stage of the buyer's journey," he explained. "By automating lead nurturing processes, we can deliver the right message to the right person at the right time, increasing engagement and moving prospects closer to conversion."

Emma, the strategist, leaned forward with anticipation. "Let's uncover the strategies for automating lead nurturing," she suggested. "We'll focus on six critical areas: segmentation and targeting, content mapping, workflow automation, lead scoring, personalization, and performance measurement."

Lisa clicked her remote, and the projector illuminated the room with a comprehensive overview of automating lead nurturing. "We'll start with segmentation and targeting," she announced.

Segmentation and Targeting

Emma emphasized the importance of segmenting leads based on their characteristics, behaviors, and interests to deliver targeted and relevant content. "Segmentation allows us to divide our leads into groups based on shared characteristics or behaviors," she explained. "By segmenting leads, we can tailor our messaging and content to their specific needs and preferences, increasing relevance and engagement."

David suggested leveraging data and analytics to identify key segments and personas and develop targeted content for each segment. "Data-driven segmentation enables us to identify patterns and trends in lead behavior and preferences," he noted. "By analyzing data such as demographics, engagement metrics, and past interactions, we can create targeted content and messaging that resonates with each segment."

Lisa highlighted the significance of workflow automation in delivering personalized and timely interactions to leads. "Workflow automation allows us to create automated sequences of actions and communications that guide leads through the buyer's journey," she remarked. "By automating repetitive tasks such as sending emails, triggering follow-up actions, and updating lead statuses, we can save time and resources while maintaining consistency and efficiency."

As the discussion continued, the team explored the intricacies of automating lead nurturing, recognizing its significance in engaging prospects, building relationships, and driving conversions. With a strategic approach to segmentation and targeting, content mapping, and workflow automation, they were poised to leverage automation to nurture leads effectively and achieve their sales and marketing objectives.

Automated Email Campaigns

In the focused environment of the InnovateTech conference room, the team delved into the crucial aspect of automated email campaigns. Lisa, Emma, David, and their colleagues recognized the pivotal role of email automation in nurturing leads, engaging customers, and driving conversions.

Lisa, the CEO, initiated the discussion with purpose. "Today, we explore the power of automated email campaigns, where technology meets communication to deliver targeted and timely messages," she declared. "Automated email campaigns allow us to deliver personalized content, nurture leads, and drive engagement, all while saving time and resources."

David, the data guru, nodded in agreement. "Email automation enables us to send the right message to the right person at the right time, based on their behavior, preferences, and stage in the buyer's journey," he explained. "By automating email campaigns, we can deliver relevant and timely content that resonates with recipients, increasing open rates, click-through rates, and conversions."

Emma, the strategist, leaned forward with anticipation. "Let's uncover the strategies for automated email campaigns," she suggested. "We'll focus on six critical areas: segmentation and targeting, personalized content, email automation workflows, A/B testing, monitoring and optimization, and performance measurement."

Lisa clicked her remote, and the projector illuminated the room with a comprehensive overview of automated email campaigns. "We'll start with segmentation and targeting," she announced.

Segmentation and Targeting

Emma emphasized the importance of segmenting email lists based on audience characteristics, behaviors, and preferences. "Segmentation allows us to divide our email list into smaller, targeted groups based on shared characteristics or interests," she explained. "By segmenting our email list, we can deliver more relevant and personalized content to recipients, increasing engagement and conversion rates."

David suggested leveraging data and analytics to identify key segments and personas and develop targeted content for each segment. "Data-driven segmentation enables us to identify patterns and trends in recipient behavior and preferences," he noted. "By analyzing data such as demographics, past interactions, and purchase history, we can create targeted email campaigns that resonate with each segment."

Lisa highlighted the significance of personalized content in driving engagement and conversions. "Personalization is key to the success of automated email campaigns," she remarked. "By delivering personalized content and messaging based on recipient preferences and behaviors, we can increase relevancy and engagement, ultimately driving conversions and sales."

As the discussion continued, the team explored the intricacies of automated email campaigns, recognizing its significance in nurturing leads, engaging customers, and driving revenue. With a strategic approach to segmentation and targeting, personalized content, and email automation workflows, they were poised to leverage email automation to achieve their sales and marketing objectives effectively.

Tracking and Measuring Automation Success

In the focused environment of the InnovateTech conference room, the team delved into the critical aspect of tracking and measuring the success of automation efforts. Lisa, Emma, David, and their colleagues recognized the importance of data-driven insights in evaluating performance and optimizing strategies.

Lisa, the CEO, initiated the discussion with purpose. "Today, we explore the importance of tracking and measuring automation success, where data meets decision-making to drive continuous improvement," she declared. "Tracking and measuring automation efforts allow us to assess performance, identify areas for optimization, and demonstrate the impact of our initiatives on business outcomes."

David, the data guru, nodded in agreement. "Data-driven insights enable us to understand how our automation efforts are performing and where improvements can be made," he explained. "By tracking key metrics and KPIs, we can evaluate the effectiveness of our strategies and make informed decisions to drive better results."

Emma, the strategist, leaned forward with anticipation. "Let's uncover the strategies for tracking and measuring automation success," she suggested. "We'll focus on six critical areas: defining metrics and KPIs, data collection and analysis, performance dashboards, A/B testing, continuous optimization, and reporting."

Lisa clicked her remote, and the projector illuminated the room with a comprehensive overview of tracking and measuring automation success. "We'll start with defining metrics and KPIs," she announced.

Defining Metrics and KPIs

Emma emphasized the importance of defining clear and relevant metrics and KPIs to track the success of automation efforts. "Metrics and KPIs should align with our business objectives and provide meaningful insights into performance," she explained. "By defining metrics such as open rates, click-through rates, conversion rates, and ROI, we can measure the impact of our automation initiatives on key business outcomes."

David suggested leveraging data and analytics tools to

collect and analyze data from automation platforms and other sources. "Data collection and analysis enable us to track and measure performance across various channels and touchpoints," he noted. "By analyzing data such as engagement metrics, customer behavior, and campaign performance, we can gain insights into what's working and what's not, and make data-driven decisions to optimize our strategies."

Lisa highlighted the importance of performance dashboards in providing real-time visibility into automation performance. "Performance dashboards allow us to monitor key metrics and KPIs in real-time, enabling us to quickly identify trends, patterns, and areas for improvement," she remarked. "By visualizing data in an easy-to-understand format, we can make informed decisions and take action to drive better results."

As the discussion continued, the team explored the intricacies of tracking and measuring automation success, recognizing its importance in driving continuous improvement and achieving business objectives. With a strategic approach to defining metrics and KPIs, data collection and analysis, and performance dashboards, they were poised to leverage data-driven insights to optimize automation strategies and drive better results.

13

Chapter 13: Managing Sales and Marketing Budgets

Allocating Resources Effectively

In the strategic atmosphere of the InnovateTech conference room, the team delved into the crucial aspect of allocating resources effectively within sales and marketing budgets. Lisa, Emma, David, and their colleagues recognized the importance of strategic resource allocation in driving success and maximizing return on investment.

Lisa, the CEO, set the stage for the discussion with determination. "Today, we explore the art of allocating resources effectively within our sales and marketing budgets, where strategic decisions meet financial stewardship to drive growth," she declared. "Effective resource allocation allows us to prioritize initiatives, optimize spending, and achieve our business objectives efficiently."

David, the data guru, nodded in agreement. "Resource allocation involves making strategic decisions about where to allocate budgetary resources to achieve the greatest impact," he explained. "By aligning spending with business goals and objectives, we can maximize ROI and drive sustainable growth."

Emma, the strategist, leaned forward with anticipation. "Let's uncover the strategies for allocating resources effectively," she suggested. "We'll focus on six critical areas: goal alignment, data-driven decision-making, prioritization, experimentation, flexibility, and performance monitoring."

Lisa clicked her remote, and the projector illuminated the room with a comprehensive overview of allocating resources effectively. "We'll start with goal alignment," she announced.

Goal Alignment

Emma emphasized the importance of aligning resource allocation decisions with overarching business goals and objectives. "Goal alignment ensures that our spending priorities are aligned with our strategic priorities," she explained. "By clearly defining our goals and objectives, we can prioritize initiatives that contribute most directly to achieving them, maximizing the impact of our investments."

David suggested leveraging data and analytics to inform resource allocation decisions. "Data-driven decision-making enables us to identify opportunities, assess risks, and optimize spending," he noted. "By analyzing data such as customer acquisition costs, lifetime value, and channel performance, we can allocate resources to initiatives with the highest potential for return on investment."

Lisa highlighted the significance of prioritization in resource allocation. "Prioritization involves identifying initiatives that offer the greatest potential for impact and allocating resources accordingly," she remarked. "By focusing on initiatives that align with our strategic priorities and have the highest potential for ROI, we can optimize our spending and drive better results."

As the discussion continued, the team explored the intricacies of allocating resources effectively within sales and marketing budgets, recognizing its importance in driving success and achieving business objectives. With a strategic approach to goal alignment, data-driven decision-making, and prioritization, they were poised to maximize the impact of their investments and drive sustainable growth.

Cost-Benefit Analysis

In the strategic ambiance of the InnovateTech conference room, the team delved into the critical aspect of conducting cost-benefit analysis within sales and marketing budgets. Lisa, Emma, David, and their colleagues understood the importance of evaluating the potential return on investment (ROI) for each expenditure.

Lisa, the CEO, set the stage for the discussion with determination. "Today, we explore the necessity of conducting cost-benefit analysis within our sales and marketing budgets, where informed decisions meet financial prudence to drive efficiency," she declared. "Cost-benefit analysis allows us to assess the potential ROI of our expenditures, ensuring that we allocate resources wisely and maximize our financial returns."

David, the data guru, nodded in agreement. "Cost-benefit analysis involves quantifying the costs and benefits associated with each expenditure to determine its potential impact on the bottom line," he explained. "By evaluating the expected return on investment for each initiative, we can prioritize spending and optimize our budget allocation to achieve our business objectives."

Emma, the strategist, leaned forward with anticipation. "Let's uncover the strategies for conducting cost-benefit analysis," she suggested. "We'll focus on six critical areas: identifying costs and benefits, quantifying impact, assessing risks, sensitivity analysis, decision-making, and performance tracking."

Lisa clicked her remote, and the projector illuminated the room with a comprehensive overview of cost-benefit analysis. "We'll start with identifying costs and benefits," she announced.

Identifying Costs and Benefits

Emma emphasized the importance of identifying and quantifying both the costs and benefits associated with each expenditure. "Costs include direct expenses such as advertising spend, personnel costs, and technology investments," she explained. "Benefits encompass the expected outcomes or returns, such as increased revenue, customer acquisition, or brand awareness."

David suggested leveraging data and analytics to quantify the potential impact of each expenditure. "Quantifying impact involves estimating the expected return on investment for each initiative," he noted. "By analyzing historical data, market trends, and performance metrics, we can make informed projections about the potential benefits of our investments."

Lisa highlighted the significance of assessing risks in cost-benefit analysis. "Assessing risks involves identifying potential obstacles or uncertainties that may impact the success of our initiatives," she remarked. "By evaluating risks such as market volatility, competitive dynamics, and regulatory changes, we can mitigate potential threats and make more informed decisions."

As the discussion continued, the team explored the intricacies of conducting cost-benefit analysis within sales and marketing budgets, recognizing its importance in driving efficiency and maximizing financial returns. With a strategic approach to identifying costs and benefits, quantifying impact, and assessing risks, they were poised to optimize their budget allocation and achieve their business objectives effectively.

ROI Measurement

In the determined ambiance of the InnovateTech conference room, the team delved into the pivotal aspect of measuring return on investment (ROI) within sales and marketing budgets. Lisa, Emma, David, and their colleagues recognized the importance of quantifying the financial returns generated by their expenditures.

Lisa, the CEO, initiated the discussion with purpose. "Today, we explore the necessity of measuring return on investment within our sales and marketing budgets, where financial insights meet performance evaluation to drive accountability," she declared. "ROI measurement allows us to assess the effectiveness of our spending, identify areas for improvement, and optimize our budget allocation to maximize returns."

David, the data guru, nodded in agreement. "ROI measurement involves quantifying the financial returns generated by our expenditures relative to the costs incurred," he explained.

"By evaluating the ROI of each initiative, we can prioritize investments that deliver the highest returns and allocate resources more effectively."

Emma, the strategist, leaned forward with anticipation. "Let's uncover the strategies for measuring ROI," she suggested. "We'll focus on six critical areas: defining ROI metrics, data collection and analysis, attribution modeling, benchmarking, performance tracking, and reporting."

Lisa clicked her remote, and the projector illuminated the room with a comprehensive overview of ROI measurement. "We'll start with defining ROI metrics," she announced.

Defining ROI Metrics

Emma emphasized the importance of defining clear and relevant metrics for measuring ROI. "ROI metrics should align with our business objectives and provide meaningful insights into the financial returns generated by our investments," she explained. "By defining metrics such as revenue generated, customer acquisition cost, lifetime value, and marketing-attributed revenue, we can accurately assess the impact of our spending on the bottom line."

David suggested leveraging data and analytics to collect and analyze data for ROI measurement. "Data collection and analysis enable us to track and measure the financial returns generated by our expenditures," he noted. "By analyzing data such as sales revenue, customer acquisition costs, and marketing attribution, we can calculate ROI and evaluate the effectiveness of our initiatives."

Lisa highlighted the significance of attribution modeling in measuring ROI accurately. "Attribution modeling allows us to attribute revenue and conversions to specific marketing initiatives or channels," she remarked. "By using advanced attribution models such as first-touch, last-touch, or multi-touch attribution, we can accurately quantify the impact of each marketing touchpoint on revenue generation and calculate ROI more effectively."

As the discussion continued, the team explored the intricacies of measuring ROI within sales and marketing budgets, recognizing its importance in driving accountability and optimizing financial returns. With a strategic approach to defining ROI metrics, data collection and analysis, and attribution modeling, they were poised to assess the effectiveness of their spending accurately and make informed decisions to drive better results.

Budgeting for Tools and Technology

In the focused atmosphere of the InnovateTech conference room, the team turned their attention to the critical aspect of budgeting for tools and technology within sales and marketing budgets. Lisa, Emma, David, and their colleagues recognized the importance of investing in the right tools and technology to drive efficiency and effectiveness.

Lisa, the CEO, initiated the discussion with determination. "Today, we explore the necessity of budgeting for tools and technology within our sales and marketing budgets, where innovation meets optimization to drive success," she declared. "Budgeting for tools and technology allows us to equip our teams with the resources they need to streamline processes, automate tasks, and drive better results."

David, the data guru, nodded in agreement. "Investing in

the right tools and technology can have a significant impact on our productivity, efficiency, and performance," he explained. "By budgeting for tools such as CRM systems, marketing automation platforms, and analytics tools, we can empower our teams to work more effectively and achieve our business objectives."

Emma, the strategist, leaned forward with anticipation. "Let's uncover the strategies for budgeting for tools and technology," she suggested. "We'll focus on six critical areas: needs assessment, research and evaluation, cost-benefit analysis, implementation planning, training and support, and performance monitoring."

Lisa clicked her remote, and the projector illuminated the room with a comprehensive overview of budgeting for tools and technology. "We'll start with needs assessment," she announced.

Needs Assessment

Emma emphasized the importance of conducting a thorough needs assessment to identify the tools and technology required to support sales and marketing initiatives. "Needs assessment involves evaluating our current processes, identifying pain points and inefficiencies, and determining the tools and technology needed to address them," she explained. "By understanding our requirements and objectives, we can prioritize investments that deliver the greatest value and impact."

David suggested conducting research and evaluation to identify potential tools and technology solutions. "Research and evaluation involve gathering information about available tools and technology solutions, assessing their features, functionality, and suitability for our needs," he noted. "By comparing different options and gathering feedback from users and experts, we can make informed decisions about which tools to invest in."

Lisa highlighted the importance of cost-benefit analysis in budgeting for tools and technology. "Cost-benefit analysis involves evaluating the expected costs and benefits associated with each tool or technology investment," she remarked. "By assessing factors such as upfront costs, ongoing expenses, and potential returns, we can prioritize investments that offer the highest value and ROI."

As the discussion continued, the team explored the intricacies of budgeting for tools and technology within sales and marketing budgets, recognizing its importance in driving efficiency, productivity, and performance. With a strategic approach to needs assessment, research and evaluation, and cost-benefit analysis, they were poised to make informed decisions about investing in the right tools and technology to support their business objectives effectively.

Balancing Short-term and Long-term Investments

In the thoughtful ambiance of the InnovateTech conference room, the team focused on the crucial aspect of balancing short-term and long-term investments within sales and marketing budgets. Lisa, Emma, David, and their colleagues understood the delicate balance required to achieve both immediate results and sustainable growth.

Lisa, the CEO, led the discussion with a clear vision. "Today, we explore the importance of balancing short-term and long-term investments within our sales and marketing budgets, where foresight meets agility to drive success," she declared. "Balancing short-term and long-term investments allows us to achieve immediate results while laying the foundation for sustained growth and competitiveness."

David, the data guru, nodded in agreement. "Investing in both short-term tactics and long-term strategies is essential for driving both immediate impact and long-term value," he explained. "By balancing short-term gains with long-term investments, we can meet current objectives while building a strong foundation for future success."

Emma, the strategist, leaned forward with anticipation. "Let's uncover the strategies for balancing short-term and long-term investments," she suggested. "We'll focus on six critical areas: goal alignment, resource allocation, risk management, innovation, scalability, and performance measurement."

Lisa clicked her remote, and the projector illuminated the room with a comprehensive overview of balancing short-term and long-term investments. "We'll start with goal alignment," she announced.

Goal Alignment

Emma emphasized the importance of aligning short-term and long-term investments with overarching business goals and objectives. "Goal alignment ensures that our investments support both immediate needs and long-term strategic objectives," she explained. "By defining clear goals and objectives, we can prioritize investments that deliver the greatest impact in the short term while laying the foundation for future growth."

David suggested that resource allocation should reflect

the balance between short-term and long-term priorities. "Resource allocation involves prioritizing investments that balance short-term gains with long-term value creation," he noted. "By allocating resources strategically, we can ensure that we have the flexibility to pursue both immediate opportunities and future growth initiatives."

Lisa highlighted the importance of managing risks associated with both short-term tactics and long-term strategies. "Risk management involves identifying potential risks and uncertainties and developing strategies to mitigate them," she remarked. "By assessing risks such as market volatility, competitive dynamics, and technology changes, we can minimize potential threats and maximize opportunities for success."

As the discussion continued, the team explored the intricacies of balancing short-term and long-term investments within sales and marketing budgets, recognizing its importance in driving both immediate results and sustainable growth. With a strategic approach to goal alignment, resource allocation, and risk management, they were poised to achieve their business objectives effectively while laying the foundation for future success.

Adjusting Budgets Based on Performance

In the focused ambiance of the InnovateTech conference room, the team addressed the critical aspect of adjusting budgets based on performance within sales and marketing budgets. Lisa, Emma, David, and their colleagues understood the importance of agility and responsiveness in optimizing budget allocation to drive better results.

Lisa, the CEO, led the discussion with a determined tone.

"Today, we explore the necessity of adjusting budgets based on performance within our sales and marketing budgets, where adaptability meets accountability to drive efficiency," she declared. "Adjusting budgets based on performance allows us to allocate resources more effectively, prioritize high-performing initiatives, and maximize our return on investment."

David, the data guru, nodded in agreement. "Monitoring performance and adjusting budgets accordingly is essential for optimizing spending and driving better results," he explained. "By reallocating resources from underperforming initiatives to high-performing ones, we can maximize our impact and achieve our business objectives more efficiently."

Emma, the strategist, leaned forward with anticipation. "Let's uncover the strategies for adjusting budgets based on performance," she suggested. "We'll focus on six critical areas: performance tracking, data analysis, decision-making, agility, flexibility, and continuous improvement."

Lisa clicked her remote, and the projector illuminated the room with a comprehensive overview of adjusting budgets based on performance. "We'll start with performance tracking," she announced.

Performance Tracking

Emma emphasized the importance of tracking performance metrics to assess the effectiveness of sales and marketing initiatives. "Performance tracking involves monitoring key metrics and KPIs to evaluate the impact of our investments," she explained. "By tracking metrics such as conversion rates, ROI, customer acquisition costs, and revenue growth, we can

CHAPTER 13: MANAGING SALES AND MARKETING BUDGETS

identify which initiatives are performing well and which ones need adjustment."

David suggested leveraging data analysis to gain insights into performance trends and patterns. "Data analysis enables us to uncover insights from performance data and identify opportunities for optimization," he noted. "By analyzing trends, patterns, and correlations in performance data, we can make informed decisions about where to allocate resources for maximum impact."

Lisa highlighted the importance of agility and flexibility in adjusting budgets based on performance. "Agility and flexibility allow us to respond quickly to changes in market conditions, customer behavior, and competitive dynamics," she remarked. "By being agile and flexible in our approach to budget allocation, we can adapt to evolving circumstances and optimize our spending to drive better results."

As the discussion continued, the team explored the intricacies of adjusting budgets based on performance within sales and marketing budgets, recognizing its importance in driving efficiency and maximizing return on investment. With a strategic approach to performance tracking, data analysis, and agility, they were poised to optimize their budget allocation and achieve their business objectives more effectively.

14

Chapter 14: Training and Development

Skills Assessment and Training Needs

In the vibrant setting of the InnovateTech conference room, the team gathered to discuss the crucial topic of training and development within the organization. Lisa, Emma, David, and their colleagues understood the importance of assessing skills and identifying training needs to nurture talent and drive growth.

Lisa, the CEO, kicked off the discussion with enthusiasm. "Today, we delve into the realm of training and development, where talent meets opportunity to foster innovation and excellence," she declared. "Skills assessment and identifying training needs are the cornerstones of our development strategy, enabling us to equip our teams with the knowledge and skills they need to succeed."

David, the data guru, nodded in agreement. "Assessing skills and identifying training needs allows us to understand our team's strengths and areas for improvement," he explained. "By providing targeted training and development opportunities, we can enhance individual and team performance, driving better results for the organization."

Emma, the strategist, leaned forward with anticipation. "Let's uncover the strategies for skills assessment and identifying training needs," she suggested. "We'll focus on six critical areas: skills gap analysis, performance reviews, employee feedback, benchmarking, industry trends, and future skills."

Lisa clicked her remote, and the projector illuminated the room with a comprehensive overview of skills assessment and training needs. "We'll start with skills gap analysis," she announced.

Skills Gap Analysis

Emma emphasized the importance of conducting a thorough skills gap analysis to identify areas where additional training and development are needed. "Skills gap analysis involves comparing the skills and competencies required for roles within the organization with the skills and competencies currently possessed by employees," she explained. "By identifying gaps between current and desired skills levels, we can prioritize training initiatives to address areas of need."

David suggested leveraging performance reviews and employee feedback to gain insights into individual and team capabilities. "Performance reviews and employee feedback provide valuable insights into strengths, weaknesses, and areas for improvement," he noted. "By soliciting feedback from employees and assessing performance against predefined competencies, we can identify specific training needs and tailor development plans accordingly."

Lisa highlighted the importance of benchmarking against industry standards and trends. "Benchmarking allows us to compare our team's skills and capabilities against industry standards and best practices," she remarked. "By staying abreast of industry trends and future skills requirements, we can proactively address emerging training needs and ensure that our team remains competitive and future-ready."

As the discussion continued, the team explored the intricacies of skills assessment and identifying training needs, recognizing its importance in nurturing talent and driving organizational success. With a strategic approach to skills gap analysis, performance reviews, and benchmarking, they were poised to develop targeted training and development initiatives that would empower their team to thrive in an ever-changing business landscape.

Sales Training Programs

In the dynamic atmosphere of the InnovateTech conference room, the team continued their discussion on training and development, focusing now on the critical area of sales training programs. Lisa, Emma, David, and their colleagues understood the pivotal role of effective sales training in equipping their teams with the skills and knowledge needed to drive revenue and foster customer relationships.

Lisa, the CEO, steered the conversation with purpose. "Now, let's delve into the realm of sales training programs, where expertise meets opportunity to enhance our sales force's effectiveness and drive business growth," she declared. "Sales training programs are essential for equipping our teams with the skills, knowledge, and techniques they need to excel in a competitive marketplace."

David, the data guru, nodded in agreement. "Effective sales training programs provide our teams with the tools and strategies they need to identify opportunities, overcome objections, and close deals," he explained. "By investing in targeted sales training initiatives, we can enhance our team's performance and drive better results for the organization."

Emma, the strategist, leaned forward with anticipation. "Let's uncover the strategies for implementing effective sales training programs," she suggested. "We'll focus on six critical areas: curriculum development, interactive learning experiences, role-playing exercises, real-world scenarios, continuous reinforcement, and performance measurement."

Lisa clicked her remote, and the projector illuminated the room with a comprehensive overview of sales training programs. "We'll start with curriculum development," she announced.

Curriculum Development

Emma emphasized the importance of developing a comprehensive curriculum that addresses the specific needs and challenges faced by the sales team. "Curriculum development involves designing training materials and resources that cover essential sales skills, techniques, and processes," she explained. "By tailoring the curriculum to address the unique requirements of our sales force, we can ensure that training programs are relevant, engaging, and effective."

David suggested incorporating interactive learning experiences to enhance engagement and retention. "Interactive learning experiences such as workshops, simulations, and gamification can make training more engaging and memorable," he noted. "By providing hands-on opportunities for practice and application, we can reinforce key concepts and improve learning outcomes."

Lisa highlighted the importance of incorporating role-playing exercises and real-world scenarios into sales training programs. "Role-playing exercises and real-world scenarios allow our teams to practice and apply their skills in a simulated environment," she remarked. "By simulating common sales situations and challenges, we can prepare our teams to handle real-world scenarios more effectively."

As the discussion continued, the team explored the intricacies of implementing effective sales training programs, recognizing its importance in equipping their teams with the skills and knowledge needed to drive revenue and foster customer relationships. With a strategic approach to curriculum development, interactive learning experiences, and real-world application, they were poised to elevate their sales force's effectiveness and drive business growth.

Marketing Certification Courses

In the energetic atmosphere of the InnovateTech conference room, the team delved deeper into the discussion on training and development, now focusing on the crucial aspect of marketing certification courses. Lisa, Emma, David, and their colleagues recognized the significance of providing structured learning opportunities to enhance marketing skills and expertise within the organization.

Lisa, the CEO, guided the conversation with determination. "Let's now explore the realm of marketing certification courses, where knowledge meets certification to elevate our marketing team's capabilities and drive strategic growth," she declared. "Marketing certification courses offer structured learning experiences that equip our team with the latest industry knowledge, best practices, and specialized skills needed to excel in their roles."

David, the data guru, nodded in agreement. "Marketing certification courses provide our team with the opportunity to gain valuable insights, acquire new skills, and earn recognized credentials in specialized areas of marketing," he explained. "By investing in certification programs, we can enhance our team's expertise, credibility, and effectiveness in driving marketing initiatives."

Emma, the strategist, leaned forward with anticipation. "Let's uncover the strategies for implementing effective marketing certification courses," she suggested. "We'll focus on six critical areas: course selection, learning objectives, certification options, study materials, exam preparation, and ongoing support."

Lisa clicked her remote, and the projector illuminated the room with a comprehensive overview of marketing certification courses. "We'll start with course selection," she announced.

Course Selection

Emma emphasized the importance of selecting marketing certification courses that align with the organization's strategic objectives and the individual career goals of team members. "Course selection involves identifying reputable certification programs that offer relevant content and recognized credentials in specialized areas of marketing," she explained. "By offering a range of certification options, we can cater to the diverse interests and career aspirations of our team members."

David suggested defining clear learning objectives for each certification course to ensure alignment with desired outcomes. "Learning objectives provide a roadmap for what team members can expect to achieve by completing a certification course," he noted. "By defining clear objectives, we can ensure that certification programs address specific skills gaps and support career advancement within the organization."

Lisa highlighted the importance of providing study materials and exam preparation resources to support team members throughout the certification process. "Study materials and exam preparation resources help team members prepare for certification exams and reinforce key concepts," she remarked. "By offering access to study guides, practice exams, and online resources, we can empower our team members to succeed in their certification journey."

As the discussion continued, the team explored the intricacies of implementing effective marketing certification courses, recognizing their importance in enhancing marketing skills and expertise within the organization. With a strategic approach to course selection, learning objectives, and exam preparation, they were poised to elevate their marketing team's capabilities and drive strategic growth through certified expertise.

Continuous Learning and Development

In the vibrant setting of the InnovateTech conference room, the team continued their exploration of training and development, now focusing on the essential aspect of continuous learning and development. Lisa, Emma, David, and their colleagues understood the critical role of ongoing education in staying competitive and driving innovation within the organization.

Lisa, the CEO, led the discussion with conviction. "Now, let's turn our attention to the concept of continuous learning and development, where growth meets evolution to cultivate a culture of excellence and innovation," she declared. "Continuous learning and development are essential for keeping our teams engaged, motivated, and equipped with the latest skills and knowledge needed to succeed in a rapidly changing business landscape."

David, the data guru, nodded in agreement. "Continuous learning and development allow our teams to stay ahead of industry trends, adapt to new technologies, and foster a culture of innovation and excellence," he explained. "By investing in ongoing education and professional development opportunities, we can empower our teams to thrive in an ever-evolving business environment."

Emma, the strategist, leaned forward with anticipation. "Let's uncover the strategies for implementing effective continuous learning and development programs," she suggested. "We'll focus on six critical areas: learning pathways, personalized development plans, mentorship programs, peer learning communities, external resources, and performance feedback."

Lisa clicked her remote, and the projector illuminated the

room with a comprehensive overview of continuous learning and development. "We'll start with learning pathways," she announced.

Learning Pathways

Emma emphasized the importance of offering structured learning pathways that align with the organization's strategic objectives and the career aspirations of team members. "Learning pathways provide a framework for continuous development, guiding team members through a curated sequence of learning experiences and skill-building activities," she explained. "By offering pathways tailored to different roles, levels, and areas of interest, we can ensure that team members have access to relevant and impactful development opportunities."

David suggested creating personalized development plans to support individual growth and career advancement. "Personalized development plans enable team members to identify their strengths, areas for improvement, and career goals," he noted. "By working with managers and mentors to create tailored development plans, team members can take ownership of their learning journey and pursue opportunities that align with their professional aspirations."

Lisa highlighted the importance of mentorship programs and peer learning communities in fostering a culture of continuous learning and development. "Mentorship programs pair team members with experienced mentors who can provide guidance, support, and feedback," she remarked. "Peer learning communities create opportunities for collaboration, knowledge sharing, and skill exchange among team members, fostering a culture of learning and innovation."

As the discussion continued, the team explored the intricacies of implementing effective continuous learning and development programs, recognizing their importance in driving engagement, motivation, and innovation within the organization. With a strategic approach to learning pathways, personalized development plans, and mentorship programs, they were poised to cultivate a culture of excellence and empower their teams to thrive in a dynamic business environment.

Leadership Development

In the spirited ambiance of the InnovateTech conference room, the team delved deeper into the discussion on training and development, now focusing on the pivotal aspect of leadership development. Lisa, Emma, David, and their colleagues understood the critical role of nurturing leadership talent to drive organizational growth and foster a culture of innovation.

Lisa, the CEO, guided the conversation with unwavering determination. "Now, let's explore the realm of leadership development, where vision meets empowerment to cultivate a new generation of leaders poised to lead our organization into the future," she declared. "Leadership development is essential for identifying and nurturing talent, building strong teams, and driving strategic growth initiatives."

David, the data guru, nodded in agreement. "Leadership development programs provide emerging leaders with the skills, knowledge, and experience they need to inspire, motivate, and guide their teams to success," he explained. "By investing in leadership development, we can ensure a pipeline of talented leaders ready to tackle the challenges of tomorrow."

Emma, the strategist, leaned forward with anticipation. "Let's uncover the strategies for implementing effective leadership development programs," she suggested. "We'll focus on six critical areas: leadership competencies, experiential learning, mentorship and coaching, feedback and assessment, succession planning, and continuous growth."

Lisa clicked her remote, and the projector illuminated the room with a comprehensive overview of leadership development. "We'll start with leadership competencies," she announced.

Leadership Competencies

Emma emphasized the importance of defining clear leadership competencies that align with the organization's values, vision, and strategic objectives. "Leadership competencies outline the skills, qualities, and behaviors expected of leaders within the organization," she explained. "By defining clear competencies, we can identify potential leaders, assess their readiness for leadership roles, and provide targeted development opportunities to support their growth."

David suggested incorporating experiential learning opportunities into leadership development programs to provide hands-on experience and real-world challenges. "Experiential learning allows emerging leaders to apply their skills and knowledge in practical settings, gain valuable experience, and develop critical leadership capabilities," he noted. "By providing opportunities for stretch assignments, cross-functional projects, and leadership roles, we can accelerate their development and prepare them for future leadership positions."

Lisa highlighted the importance of mentorship and coaching in supporting leadership development. "Mentorship and coaching programs pair emerging leaders with experienced mentors who can provide guidance, support, and feedback," she remarked. "By offering personalized coaching and mentoring, we can help emerging leaders navigate challenges, develop their leadership style, and unlock their full potential."

As the discussion continued, the team explored the intricacies of implementing effective leadership development programs, recognizing their importance in cultivating a new generation of leaders poised to drive organizational growth and foster a culture of innovation. With a strategic approach to leadership competencies, experiential learning, and mentorship programs, they were poised to nurture leadership talent and build a strong foundation for future success.

Evaluating Training Effectiveness

In the dynamic atmosphere of the InnovateTech conference room, the team approached the final aspect of their discussion on training and development: evaluating training effectiveness. Lisa, Emma, David, and their colleagues understood the importance of assessing the impact of training initiatives to ensure that investments in employee development yield tangible results for the organization.

Lisa, the CEO, led the discussion with a focused demeanor. "Now, let's turn our attention to evaluating training effectiveness, where insight meets action to optimize our learning initiatives and drive continuous improvement," she declared. "Evaluating training effectiveness allows us to assess the impact of our training programs, identify areas for improvement, and make data-driven decisions to enhance the effectiveness of future initiatives."

David, the data guru, nodded in agreement. "Evaluating training effectiveness provides valuable insights into the outcomes and impact of our training initiatives," he explained. "By collecting and analyzing data on key performance metrics, we can measure the success of our programs, identify areas for improvement, and make informed decisions to optimize our training investments."

Emma, the strategist, leaned forward with anticipation. "Let's uncover the strategies for evaluating training effectiveness," she suggested. "We'll focus on six critical areas: defining evaluation criteria, collecting feedback, measuring learning outcomes, assessing behavior change, evaluating business impact, and continuous improvement."

Lisa clicked her remote, and the projector illuminated the room with a comprehensive overview of evaluating training effectiveness. "We'll start with defining evaluation criteria," she announced.

Defining Evaluation Criteria

Emma emphasized the importance of establishing clear evaluation criteria to assess the effectiveness of training initiatives. "Evaluation criteria outline the specific outcomes and objectives that we aim to achieve through our training programs," she explained. "By defining clear criteria for success, we can ensure that our evaluation efforts are focused, relevant, and aligned with organizational goals."

David suggested collecting feedback from participants to

gain insights into their learning experience and satisfaction with the training program. "Collecting feedback allows us to understand participants' perceptions, preferences, and suggestions for improvement," he noted. "By soliciting feedback through surveys, interviews, and focus groups, we can gather valuable insights to inform future training initiatives and enhance the overall learning experience."

Lisa highlighted the importance of measuring learning outcomes to assess the extent to which participants have acquired new knowledge and skills. "Measuring learning outcomes involves assessing participants' knowledge, skills, and competencies before and after the training program," she remarked. "By administering pre- and post-training assessments, we can measure learning gains and determine the effectiveness of our training interventions."

As the discussion continued, the team explored the intricacies of evaluating training effectiveness, recognizing its importance in driving continuous improvement and maximizing the return on investment in employee development. With a strategic approach to defining evaluation criteria, collecting feedback, and measuring learning outcomes, they were poised to assess the impact of their training initiatives and make data-driven decisions to optimize future programs.

15

Chapter 15: Measuring Success and Scaling Up

Setting Benchmarks and Milestones

In the bustling ambiance of the InnovateTech conference room, the team gathered to explore the final chapter of their journey: measuring success and scaling up. Lisa, Emma, David, and their colleagues understood the importance of setting benchmarks and milestones to track progress and drive organizational growth.

Lisa, the CEO, set the tone for the discussion with a sense of purpose. "Now, let's delve into the realm of measuring success and scaling up, where ambition meets accountability to propel our organization to new heights of achievement," she declared. "Setting benchmarks and milestones is essential for monitoring progress, identifying areas for improvement, and charting a course for future success."

David, the data guru, nodded in agreement. "Setting benchmarks and milestones provides a framework for measuring progress and evaluating the effectiveness of our growth initiatives," he explained. "By defining clear targets and timelines, we can track our performance against key metrics, identify deviations from our goals, and take corrective action as needed."

Emma, the strategist, leaned forward with anticipation. "Let's uncover the strategies for setting benchmarks and milestones," she suggested. "We'll focus on six critical areas: goal alignment, SMART objectives, key performance indicators, tracking mechanisms, periodic reviews, and course correction."

Lisa clicked her remote, and the projector illuminated the room with a comprehensive overview of setting benchmarks and milestones. "We'll start with goal alignment," she announced.

Goal Alignment

Emma emphasized the importance of aligning benchmarks and milestones with the organization's strategic goals and objectives. "Goal alignment ensures that benchmarks and milestones are directly linked to the organization's overarching vision and mission," she explained. "By aligning our growth initiatives with strategic priorities, we can focus our efforts on activities that drive meaningful progress and create value for the organization."

David suggested using SMART objectives to set specific, measurable, achievable, relevant, and time-bound benchmarks and milestones. "SMART objectives provide a framework for setting clear, actionable targets that are aligned with organizational goals," he noted. "By ensuring that benchmarks and milestones are SMART, we can establish a roadmap for success and track our progress with precision."

Lisa highlighted the importance of defining key performance indicators (KPIs) to measure progress and evaluate success. "Key performance indicators allow us to quantify our progress and assess the effectiveness of our growth initiatives," she remarked. "By selecting KPIs that are relevant, actionable, and aligned with strategic objectives, we can monitor our performance and make data-driven decisions to drive continuous improvement."

As the discussion continued, the team explored the intricacies of setting benchmarks and milestones, recognizing their importance in driving organizational growth and success. With a strategic approach to goal alignment, SMART objectives, and key performance indicators, they were poised to chart a course for future success and scale up their operations to new heights of achievement.

Continuous Improvement Processes

In the vibrant atmosphere of the InnovateTech conference room, the team continued their exploration of measuring success and scaling up, now focusing on the vital aspect of continuous improvement processes. Lisa, Emma, David, and their colleagues understood the importance of fostering a culture of continuous improvement to drive innovation and sustain organizational growth.

Lisa, the CEO, set the stage for the discussion with unwavering determination. "Now, let's delve into the realm of continuous improvement processes, where innovation meets iteration to propel our organization forward on a path of sustained success," she declared. "Continuous improvement processes are essential for identifying opportunities for enhancement, optimizing our operations, and fostering a culture of innovation and excellence."

David, the data guru, nodded in agreement. "Continuous improvement processes provide a systematic approach to identifying, prioritizing, and implementing improvements across our organization," he explained. "By embracing a culture of continuous improvement, we can empower our teams to innovate, adapt to change, and drive organizational excellence."

Emma, the strategist, leaned forward with anticipation. "Let's uncover the strategies for implementing effective continuous improvement processes," she suggested. "We'll focus on six critical areas: root cause analysis, process mapping, feedback mechanisms, experimentation and innovation, performance monitoring, and iterative refinement."

Lisa clicked her remote, and the projector illuminated the room with a comprehensive overview of continuous improvement processes. "We'll start with root cause analysis," she announced.

Root Cause Analysis

Emma emphasized the importance of conducting root cause analysis to identify the underlying factors contributing to issues and inefficiencies within the organization. "Root cause analysis allows us to uncover the underlying causes of problems and inefficiencies, rather than just addressing symptoms," she explained. "By identifying root causes, we can implement targeted solutions that address the underlying issues and prevent recurrence."

David suggested using process mapping techniques to visualize and understand the flow of activities within the organization. "Process mapping provides a visual representation of our workflows, allowing us to identify bottlenecks, redundancies, and areas for improvement," he noted. "By mapping our processes, we can streamline operations, improve efficiency, and enhance the overall effectiveness of our organization."

Lisa highlighted the importance of establishing feedback mechanisms to solicit input and ideas from employees at all levels of the organization. "Feedback mechanisms provide a platform for employees to share their insights, suggestions, and concerns," she remarked. "By fostering a culture of open communication and feedback, we can harness the collective wisdom of our team members to drive continuous improvement and innovation."

As the discussion continued, the team explored the intricacies of implementing effective continuous improvement processes, recognizing their importance in driving innovation, optimizing operations, and sustaining organizational growth. With a strategic approach to root cause analysis, process mapping, and feedback mechanisms, they were poised to foster a culture of continuous improvement and propel their organization forward on a path of sustained success.

Scaling Sales Operations

In the dynamic setting of the InnovateTech conference room, the team continued their discussion on measuring success and scaling up, now shifting their focus to the critical aspect of scaling sales operations. Lisa, Emma, David, and their

CHAPTER 15: MEASURING SUCCESS AND SCALING UP

colleagues understood the importance of expanding sales capabilities to drive revenue growth and capitalize on emerging opportunities.

Lisa, the CEO, directed the conversation with a sense of purpose. "Now, let's explore the realm of scaling sales operations, where expansion meets execution to fuel our growth and propel us towards our strategic objectives," she declared. "Scaling sales operations is essential for increasing market penetration, reaching new customers, and driving revenue growth."

David, the data guru, nodded in agreement. "Scaling sales operations involves expanding our sales capabilities to accommodate growth and capitalize on new opportunities," he explained. "By optimizing our sales processes, leveraging technology, and expanding our sales team, we can increase our capacity to serve customers and drive revenue."

Emma, the strategist, leaned forward with anticipation. "Let's uncover the strategies for scaling sales operations," she suggested. "We'll focus on six critical areas: sales process optimization, technology integration, talent acquisition and development, territory expansion, customer segmentation, and performance tracking."

Lisa clicked her remote, and the projector illuminated the room with a comprehensive overview of scaling sales operations. "We'll start with sales process optimization," she announced.

Sales Process Optimization

Emma emphasized the importance of streamlining and optimizing sales processes to improve efficiency and effectiveness. "Sales process optimization involves identifying and eliminating bottlenecks, redundancies, and inefficiencies in our sales processes," she explained. "By streamlining our processes, we can reduce friction, improve productivity, and enhance the overall customer experience."

David suggested integrating technology solutions to automate repetitive tasks and streamline sales workflows. "Technology integration allows us to leverage automation, data analytics, and artificial intelligence to optimize our sales operations," he noted. "By implementing CRM systems, sales enablement tools, and predictive analytics solutions, we can empower our sales team to work more efficiently and effectively."

Lisa highlighted the importance of talent acquisition and development in scaling sales operations. "Talent acquisition and development involve recruiting, training, and retaining top sales talent to support our growth objectives," she remarked. "By investing in recruiting efforts, onboarding programs, and ongoing training initiatives, we can build a high-performing sales team capable of driving revenue growth."

As the discussion continued, the team explored the intricacies of scaling sales operations, recognizing its importance in driving revenue growth and achieving strategic objectives. With a strategic approach to sales process optimization, technology integration, and talent acquisition, they were poised to expand their sales capabilities and capitalize on new opportunities for growth.

Expanding Marketing Efforts

In the energetic atmosphere of the InnovateTech conference room, the team transitioned to the discussion of expanding marketing efforts, a crucial aspect of their journey towards scaling up. Lisa, Emma, David, and their colleagues recognized the pivotal role of marketing in driving brand awareness, customer acquisition, and revenue growth.

Lisa, the CEO, steered the conversation with confidence. "Now, let's dive into the realm of expanding marketing efforts, where creativity meets strategy to elevate our brand presence and reach new audiences," she declared. "Expanding marketing efforts is essential for increasing market share, generating leads, and nurturing customer relationships."

David, the data guru, nodded in agreement. "Expanding marketing efforts involves deploying a mix of strategies and tactics to engage target audiences, drive traffic, and generate demand for our products and services," he explained. "By leveraging digital channels, content marketing, and targeted campaigns, we can expand our reach and attract new customers."

Emma, the strategist, leaned forward with anticipation. "Let's uncover the strategies for expanding marketing efforts," she suggested. "We'll focus on six critical areas: digital marketing strategies, content creation and distribution, audience targeting and segmentation, lead generation tactics, brand partnerships, and performance measurement."

Lisa clicked her remote, and the projector illuminated the room with a comprehensive overview of expanding marketing efforts. "We'll start with digital marketing strategies," she announced.

Digital Marketing Strategies

Emma emphasized the importance of leveraging digital channels to reach and engage target audiences. "Digital marketing strategies involve using online platforms and channels, such as social media, search engines, and email, to promote our brand, products, and services," she explained. "By leveraging digital channels, we can reach a wider audience, track performance, and optimize our marketing efforts in real-time."

David suggested focusing on content creation and distribution to provide value and engage audiences across various touchpoints. "Content creation and distribution involve producing high-quality, relevant content that resonates with our target audience and distributing it through various channels," he noted. "By creating compelling content that educates, entertains, or inspires, we can attract and retain the attention of our audience and drive them towards conversion."

Lisa highlighted the importance of audience targeting and segmentation in tailoring marketing efforts to specific demographics, interests, and behaviors. "Audience targeting and segmentation allow us to identify and prioritize high-value segments and tailor our messaging and offers to resonate with their needs and preferences," she remarked. "By segmenting our audience and delivering personalized experiences, we can increase relevance, engagement, and conversion rates."

As the discussion continued, the team explored the intricacies of expanding marketing efforts, recognizing its importance in driving brand awareness, customer acquisition, and revenue growth. With a strategic approach to digital marketing strategies, content creation, and audience targeting, they were poised to expand their reach, attract new customers, and achieve their growth objectives.

Analyzing Growth Metrics

In the charged atmosphere of the InnovateTech conference room, the team shifted their focus to analyzing growth metrics, a pivotal aspect of their journey towards scaling up. Lisa, Emma, David, and their colleagues recognized the critical importance of data-driven insights in guiding strategic decisions and fueling sustainable growth.

Lisa, the CEO, led the discussion with unwavering determination. "Now, let's delve into the realm of analyzing growth metrics, where data meets insight to illuminate our path forward and drive informed decision-making," she declared. "Analyzing growth metrics is essential for understanding our performance, identifying trends, and optimizing our strategies for sustained success."

David, the data guru, nodded in agreement. "Analyzing growth metrics involves tracking and evaluating key performance indicators (KPIs) to assess our progress and performance across various aspects of our business," he explained. "By monitoring growth metrics, we can identify areas of strength, pinpoint opportunities for improvement, and make data-driven decisions to drive our growth agenda."

Emma, the strategist, leaned forward with anticipation. "Let's uncover the strategies for analyzing growth metrics," she suggested. "We'll focus on six critical areas: defining relevant KPIs, establishing benchmarks, conducting regular performance reviews, identifying trends and patterns, conducting root cause analysis, and leveraging insights for strategic decision-making."

Lisa clicked her remote, and the projector illuminated the room with a comprehensive overview of analyzing growth metrics. "We'll start with defining relevant KPIs," she announced.

Defining Relevant KPIs

Emma emphasized the importance of defining key performance indicators (KPIs) that align with organizational goals and objectives. "Defining relevant KPIs allows us to measure progress and performance across critical areas of our business," she explained. "By selecting KPIs that are specific, measurable, actionable, relevant, and time-bound, we can establish a clear framework for tracking our growth and assessing our success."

David suggested establishing benchmarks to provide context and comparison for evaluating performance against targets and industry standards. "Establishing benchmarks allows us to gauge our performance relative to historical data, competitors, and industry averages," he noted. "By benchmarking our performance, we can identify areas of strength and weakness, set realistic targets, and strive for continuous improvement."

Lisa highlighted the importance of conducting regular performance reviews to track progress and identify opportunities for optimization. "Regular performance reviews allow us to assess our performance against targets, review progress towards strategic objectives, and identify areas for improvement," she remarked. "By conducting performance reviews on a periodic basis, we can stay agile, responsive, and focused on driving our growth agenda."

As the discussion continued, the team explored the intricacies of analyzing growth metrics, recognizing its importance in guiding strategic decisions and driving sustainable growth. With a strategic approach to defining relevant KPIs, establishing benchmarks, and conducting regular performance reviews, they were poised to harness the power of data-driven insights to achieve their growth objectives and propel their organization forward on a path of sustained success.

Long-term Strategy and Vision

In the bustling atmosphere of the InnovateTech conference room, the team embarked on the final leg of their journey through Chapter 15, focusing on the paramount aspect of long-term strategy and vision. Lisa, Emma, David, and their colleagues understood the significance of crafting a clear and compelling vision to guide their organization's trajectory towards sustainable growth.

Lisa, the CEO, set the tone for the discussion with a steadfast demeanor. "Now, let's delve into the realm of long-term strategy and vision, where foresight meets ambition to chart our course towards enduring success," she declared. "Crafting a long-term strategy and vision is essential for aligning our efforts, inspiring our teams, and navigating the complexities of an ever-changing business landscape."

David, the data guru, nodded in agreement. "A clear and compelling vision serves as a North Star, guiding our decisions and actions as we pursue our long-term objectives," he explained. "By articulating a bold vision for the future, we can inspire our teams, attract top talent, and rally stakeholders around a shared sense of purpose and direction."

Emma, the strategist, leaned forward with anticipation. "Let's uncover the strategies for crafting a long-term strategy and vision," she suggested. "We'll focus on six critical areas: environmental scanning, scenario planning, strategic foresight, goal setting, stakeholder engagement, and communication."

Lisa clicked her remote, and the projector illuminated the room with a comprehensive overview of long-term strategy and vision. "We'll start with environmental scanning," she announced.

Environmental Scanning

Emma emphasized the importance of conducting environmental scanning to assess the internal and external factors shaping the business landscape. "Environmental scanning involves monitoring and analyzing trends, developments, and disruptions in the market, industry, and broader operating environment," she explained. "By understanding the forces at play, we can anticipate opportunities and threats, adapt to change, and position ourselves for long-term success."

David suggested using scenario planning techniques to envision alternative futures and prepare for uncertainty. "Scenario planning allows us to explore different future scenarios, assess their potential impact on our business, and develop strategies to mitigate risks and capitalize on opportunities," he noted. "By considering multiple scenarios, we can enhance our resilience, flexibility, and preparedness for the unknown."

Lisa highlighted the importance of strategic foresight in shaping the organization's long-term strategy and vision. "Strategic foresight involves thinking critically and creatively about the future, envisioning possibilities, and identifying emerging trends and opportunities," she remarked. "By embracing strategic foresight, we can anticipate change, stay ahead of the curve, and position ourselves as industry leaders in the years to come."

As the discussion continued, the team explored the intricacies of crafting a long-term strategy and vision, recognizing its importance in guiding their organization towards enduring success. With a strategic approach to environmental scanning, scenario planning, and strategic foresight, they were poised to navigate the complexities of the business landscape and realize their vision for the future.

About the Author

Goodson Mumba is a multifaceted individual known for his diverse expertise and prolific contributions across various fields. As an infopreneur, thought leader, and spiritual leader, he has inspired countless individuals through his insightful teachings and impactful writings. Mumba is also an accomplished author, with several notable works to his name, including "Understanding Corporate Worship," "The Years I Spent in a Week," "Management By Harmony," "The CEO's Diary," "Change to Change" and "Creative Thinking for results" His literary works span topics ranging from business management to personal development and spirituality, reflecting his broad range of interests and insights.

With a Master of Business Leadership (MBL) and a Bachelor of Arts in Theology (BTh), Mumba brings a unique blend of business acumen and spiritual wisdom to his work. His educational background is further enriched by a Group Diploma in Management Studies, providing him with a solid foundation in organizational dynamics and leadership principles. Additionally, Mumba holds diplomas in Education

Psychology, Leadership and Management Styles, Organizational Behaviour, Financial Accounting, Economic Growth and Development, and Project Management, showcasing his commitment to continuous learning and professional development.

Mumba's expertise extends beyond traditional academic disciplines, encompassing areas such as Neuro-Linguistic Programming (NLP) and Positive Psychology. His diverse skill set is complemented by a range of certifications, including Creative Problem Solving and Decision Making, Life Coaching Fundamentals and Techniques, Professional Life Coaching, and Performance Management System Design. These certifications reflect Mumba's dedication to equipping himself with the tools and knowledge necessary to empower others and drive positive change.

As an author, Mumba's writings reflect his deep understanding of human nature, organizational dynamics, and spiritual principles. His works offer practical insights, actionable strategies, and inspirational guidance for individuals seeking personal growth, professional success, and spiritual fulfillment. Mumba's holistic approach to life and leadership resonates with readers worldwide, making him a respected figure in both the business and spiritual communities.

Overall, Goodson Mumba's diverse background, extensive knowledge, and profound insights make him a sought-after speaker, mentor, and author. His commitment to excellence, lifelong learning, and service to others continues to inspire individuals to unlock their full potential and lead lives of purpose and significance.

Goodson Mumba is renowned for initiating the concept of Management by Harmony, revolutionizing traditional management practices with a focus on balanced and holistic approaches. He has authored two influential books on this subject: "Introduction to Management by Harmony" and its sequel, "Management by Harmony."

Mumba's work has significantly impacted the field, offering innovative strategies for fostering organizational harmony and efficiency. His contributions continue to shape contemporary management theories and practices.

www.ingramcontent.com/pod-product-compliance
Lightning Source LLC
Chambersburg PA
CBHW071826210526
45479CB00001B/6